THE AWAKENING

A GUIDE FOR THOSE THAT CARRY THE LIGHT

RHONI "GENESIS" LE

Copyright © 2020 by Rhonissia L. Good

All rights reserved. This book or any portion thereof
may not be reproduced or used in any manner whatsoever
without the express written permission of the publisher
except for the use of brief quotations in a book review.

Printed in the United States of America

Library of Congress Cataloging-in-Publication Data

First Printing, 2020

ISBN 978-0-578-66380-7

ISBN 979-8-628-54197-5

www.RLHealingStudio.com

HealingwithRhonile@gmail.com

Youtube: The Naked Medium

IG: RhoniLe_The_Healing_Medium

DEDICATION

This book is dedicated to my children, my earthly guides. Without you, I wouldn't have gathered the courage to embrace my gift and purpose. Being an example for all of you is what pushed me to walk in my truth

TABLE OF CONTENTS

INTRODUCTION

Chapter 1- The Awakening......................…...1

Chapter 2- The Soul Awakening.................7

Chapter 3- The Mind Awakening.............. 14

Chapter 4- The Body Awakening................20

Chapter 5- Spirit................................... 25

Chapter 6- Frequency............................33

Chapter 7- Spiritual Senses......................41

Chapter 8- Spiritual Gifts........................49

Chapter 9- Dreams & Symbols................ 55

Chapter 10- Spiritual Maintenance............61

Chapter 11- The Prophecy.................. 71

WorkBook 75

About the Author

INTRODUCTION

Yesterday, your thoughts were different. Yesterday you lived your life like everyone else. Everything that you believed in, you now question. The food that you enjoyed is no longer appeasing. The people you built relationships with, no longer understand you. The system you had faith in has now unraveled, as layers of deception have fallen. You can feel that there is something different about you. Have you experienced vivid dreams and an interest in spirituality? What about your sensitivity to energy? Even though you may be feeling like you're losing it, there is a good explanation as to what is happening. Most likely, you're experiencing a Spiritual Awakening.

There is an energy in the air that is felt deeply by those just like you. The people that have always felt a calling to do something that would help Humanity in some way. I call them, "Those That Carry the Light." The ones that were sent here to assist in the most profound shift of consciousness. I was first given instruction from spirit to write this book in 2013. My assignment, as I call it, came through my prophetic dreams and meditation sessions very frequent and consistently for years. Spirit instructed me to write a manual for those that would help change the world and be present for a new beginning. In 2018, dreams of global destruction, illness and economic eflation became very intense. I began to prepare my family for some type of disaster while still trying to maintain my daily life. As my dreams picked up, the message that I was sent to deliver became more clear. This book was completed in Dec, 2019, and after typing the last paragraph I decided to push it aside, and release it whenever I felt it was needed. My plans and spirits agenda was not in alignment and after a major wake up call at the beginning of 2020, I uploaded my manuscript. There was a heavy rush on my spirit to get this book out for not what is happenig in the current state of the world but for what is still yet to come. This book is not written to cause panic, this is a book for those that are experiencing an awakening, so that they may prepare themselves and others for a major shift in the way we live, think and behave as humans. The souls of millions have sent out an energetic calling for us all to consciously wake up, change our ways, connect with our true selves and lead others to do the same. Those that carry the light are vital to this world and the transformation that is occuring. This book was written to help people understand what is happening during their awakening. Not only will these words bring understanding, but you will also know why you have been awakened and how significant your presence is. There is no such thing as a coincidence; if you are reading this, your Spirit led you here.

You did not imagine the messages in your mind or the feelings in your gut. What you know deep in the pit of your soul is real. You have been called to do something great. Your spiritual awakening has come upon you, and the light torch that you carry has been lit. This world is being swallowed by darkness and people are lost and abandoning all forms of hope. It is only by your light that you can heal and assist others to do the same. Now is the time to starve the ego and feed the Spirit so that you can raise your torch and lead others down the path of light. All things happen in Divine timing, and the timing is now.

THE AWAKENING

A Cherokee elder is teaching his grandson about life. "A fight is going on inside me," he said to the boy. "It is a terrible fight and it is between two wolves. One is evil — he is anger, envy, sorrow, regret, greed, arrogance, self-pity, guilt, resentment, inferiority, lies, false pride, and superiority. He continued, "The other is good — he is joy, peace, love, hope, serenity, humility, kindness, benevolence, empathy, generosity, truth, compassion, and faith. The same fight is going on inside you — and inside every other person, too."

The grandson thought about it for a minute and then asked his grandfather, "Which wolf will win?"

The old Cherokee simply replied, "The one you feed." - Anonymous

More than just a trend, and more significant than anything we have experienced here, in the physical realm is the Spiritual Awakening movement. A shift in consciousness is the result of this awakening, and it is happening to all types of people from various backgrounds, cultures, and spiritual beliefs. The awakening is occurring due to a threat to humanity. Although challenging, this awakening is an opportunity for us all to unite and work towards common goals of freedom, self-awareness, survival, and a connection with the Divine. We have been called to see the truth in ourselves and the world, in order for us to unite and rise up against the conditioning of our society that is causing the spiritual death of millions.

Everyone's awakening call is aligned with their soul's purpose and divine timing. There is a signal sent out during an awakening. This signal is sent through your spiritual DNA by our Divine creator(s), your actual and eldest ancestors. The effect of the call is the awareness of the spirit self, which triggers consciousness. The conscious awakening process pushes the spirit into the forefront and knocks it out of sleep mode. Very similar to a robot, when the power switch is turned on, awareness of the self is activated. When the spirit is propelled into the driver's seat, it will have a ripple effect on every other part of the mind & body, which will be discussed in further chapters. The awakening brings forth a part of you that has been lying dormant in the background, awaiting its return.

The soul is not new, for many have traveled many lifetimes over to arrive at this point of existence and assist in this shift. During the awakening, you will experience memories that may seem displaced and connections with strangers that feel familiar. What appears to be random dreams, visions in past life regression and deja-vu are all your memories flooding to the surface. Old souls are back and with them comes knowledge, spiritual abilities, and experiences from past lifetimes that will be necessary during this journey.

The onset of a Spiritual Awakening can vary from person to person. Traumatic events, loss, active seeking, healing, psychedelics, and even hypnosis can trigger an awakening. Many people on social media like to paint the false narrative that a spiritual awakening is like an organic feast in the jungles of Hawaii. The truth is, a spiritual awakening can be very painful and challenging, due to the destruction of deep programming. It is through deprogramming the ego and shedding the attachments, that will allow the spirit self to take control. Removing the ego from the driver's seat requires a lot of change and transformations that may feel unbearable at times. The more we learn to let go and submit to the transformation, the less painful the process will be. Letting go of the conditioning requires an open space for healing and truth. No matter how difficult the healing process is, we must rise up and complete the task at hand. Our egos feed the belly of evil and as long as the ego is running the show, evil will continue to dominate.

The ego is an anchor to the destructive programming of humans. The ego is what I like to call; the alter ego of the soul. Created to navigate in the physical realm and adapt to society, the ego, grew more prominent and out of control than it should have. People create an alter ego to give them something they do not have, in order to fulfill a goal. Beyonce created Sasha Fierce to bring forth confidence and sex appeal in order to enhance her performance. Once Beyonce was secure in her position and confident on her own, she destroyed Sasha Fierce. Just like Beyonce, we created and fed our egos to fill a void of what we felt we did not have. Not only were we feeding the ego, but so was society, and that is where we lost control.

Having to be raised by parents fully engulfed in their egos, started the process of conditioning. Years later, before even getting comfortable with "self", the school system jumped in and added to the programming. Twelve years of brainwashing the ego is all it takes to create an obedient servant. By the time high school ended, the anchor of the ego was so deeply rooted and programmed. With awareness of the soul abandoned, the ego was driven into the leadership position. From the moment of your arrival, a whole system was waiting nearby to remove your light of truth and trade it for darkness. We were all born into sin, missing the mark of the truth and light.

Currently, our world is dismantling before our eyes and partly due to the negligence and abuse from humanity. It is easy to point the finger at the evils that exist outside. It takes courage to profess the darkness that has been fed within. Evil does exist, by its own source and by what we have all taken part in creating. The truth is we have aided the darkness in flooding this planet by actively pushing it into this world or by idly standing by and allowing it to grow. When we feed the shadow parts of ourselves, we create a beast that feeds off of and produces more darkness. Our world is filled with corruption, lies, hate, and greed to state the least. Without an expanded awareness of self and a connection to the divine, we cannot make the necessary changes to our personal lives and the world we inhabit. One cannot see the light if they are blinded by total darkness. In order to create a new structure, the rotted foundation must be uprooted and destroyed. Without the awakened ones, the new structure will be just as tainted as the old.

*Poverty   *Tainted water *Mass shootings *Pedophilia *Sex-Trafficking *Homelessness *Pollution *Mental- Illness *Government Corruption *Hunger *Greed *Corrupt police forces *Rape   *Sexual abuse

*High suicide rates   *Systemic racism *Housing Crisis *Toxic food *Chemtrails *Conflict Wars *Climate Change *Religious conflicts *War *Broken families *Poor Health Care *Inequality *High taxes *The   stripping   of   Human   Rights   *Politicaly   charged   Violence *Pandemics *Drug Epidemics

The list of reasons why humanity is suffering could go on for many chapters. For all these reasons and more, we are being awakened. Just to think, everything that we see will only get worse. We are at war and for too long, humanity has tried to ignore and outrun the problems of this world but no longer does anyone have the luxury or right to do so. Why you? Why me? What could we possibly do to help?

Our planet is ill, and in order for her to survive, she must heat up and kill off all invading microbes. The temperature of our planet will be unbearable and debilitating to its inhabitants. Look around and see the symptoms of our earth fighting for its survival. As we pollute her with hate, she will strike back with illness. When humanity takes over the land and mistreats it, she will bring storms to detox her body of their greed. When purity is threatened, mother earth will spark fires to burn off that which breeds darkness. The rumble and shaking of the land is our planet regurgitating until all that causes her harm is removed. Destruction is the Divine, cleaning house. We are either on the side of what brings good health or the side of the disease. There is no lukewarm in this battle. We, the chosen, are called to assist Mother Earth in the process of elimination before all of humanity is exterminated.

To aid in the process of elimination, we must first seek the problem, dissect the symptoms, start a regimen of healing, and then create a platform for change. Let us view a measure of hate as an example. Racism is hatred. The soul does not create such a degenerate mindset. Therefore, racism is created in the ego and strengthened by wicked programming. Racism stems from fear, the fear of being left out, and the fear of not being good enough. Programming from the media, educational system, fearful parents all aid in the fears manifesting into hateful action, which is just a temper tantrum. Temper tantrums occur in individuals that cannot express their needs or control their emotions when they are frustrated and afraid; therefore, they become disruptive. When a child acts out in fear, you don't continue to judge them, for no solution comes from pointing the finger. When we see the root cause, we focus our attention on dismantling the fear by heading straight for the ego.

There is only one thing that knocks the ego off its game and that is, the soul. Your true self does not play the games set by the ego, the soul seeks transformation and peace when a situation is not aligned with its mission. To focus on healing the solution, one cannot continue to feed the ego. To find a cure for any illness, action and seeking solutions is where the energy must flow. If the good outweighs the bad, then the bad grows weak and loses power. The awakened are not here to passively wait for things to transform; our position is to act aggressively in building platforms for change.

THE AWAKENING

If Hate is the Disease, the Awakened must create Love

If Poverty is the Disease, the Awakened must create opportunities for wealth

If Pedophilia is the Disease, the Awakened must protect the children

If Hunger is the Disease, the Awakened must feed the poor

If Greed is the Disease, the Awakened must practice generosity

If A housing shortage is the Disease, the Awakened must learn to build

If Poisoned food is the Disease, the Awakened must grow their own

If Division is the Disease, the Awakened must stand united

If a Corrupt Government is the Disease, the Awakened must create their own

If an Unjust Army is the Disease, the Awakened must create and train their own soldiers

If the System is the Disease, the Awakened must dismantle it

There will never be Freedom until it is created by those enslaved. We live in a society that has been overtaken and operated by the beast of evil, created by sick egos. The reason the beast is so strong is that we have helped to feed it. The only way to bring back balance and divine order is to withdraw our participation and create the opposite of what evil has built. The awakening is not a badge of recognition to feed the ego. This Spiritual Awakening is an army of soldiers drafted by the creator to serve a divine purpose. We have not been called to update our social media status to "woke", we have been called to RISE UP & FIGHT!

THE SOUL AWAKENING

Now that we have discussed the Awakening, let us take some time to get clear about the higher self. In this chapter, it is essential to outline the relationship with the higher self and better define exactly what that is. There are many ways to connect with the inner spirit, and there are also things that break the connection that is very important for us to discuss. Just like taking a road trip, our souls needed a car to use in order to navigate through this human experience. The physical body is the chosen vehicle used to make it from one end of this journey to the next. However, just like a car, there is always someone operating behind the wheel.

Higher self is a term used to describe the eternal and intelligent being within; one's true self. To keep it simple, the higher self is the spirit that lives within each human vessel; driving the car on this road trip here in this Physical Realm. When we descend here in the physical, we are not just dropped off without any instruction or guidance as to what to do. Many people, however, believe that we are left alone to wander and figure things out on our own accord. The truth is, the higher self carries with it the map of where we are going and why. Being disconnected from our inner spirit is what causes the feelings of abandonment and uncertainty. As we continue the process of allowing the soul to run the show, we will grow accustomed to its needs, demands, and guidance over our lives. It is the higher self that bridges the connection with our creator, for our spirit in it's pure form, is a direct extension of the Divine. With that connection comes clarity, guidance, protection, and a sense of inner peace that nothing in the physical realm can give. It is the connection with the higher self that leads to encountering experiences, people, opportunities, and lessons that uplift and catapults it's subject toward spiritual growth.

Not communicating with the higher self is like taking a trip with no itinerary or GPS. The higher self carries the knowledge of the human experience and understanding of the journey. In order to allow the spirit to remain in control, one must feed and build a relationship of trust with the spirit self. Limited connection with the higher self increases connection with the ego. Allowing the ego to remain in control, will make it impossible to move beyond the social programming and conditioning, one seeks to shed. Understanding the concept of being a spirit having a human experience, the importance of staying connected to the soul remains clear. Losing touch with the higher self means going into the jungle with no food, no map, and no knowledge of the terrain.

During a spiritual awakening, one will be called to dive deeper into their being to find out who they authentically are. It is through this journey of awakening that one discovers their true self and leans on that intelligence source to heal and shed what does not serve well in the journey ahead. It was Gandhi that said, "You must be the change you want to see in the world." If we transform ourselves, there will be an automatic domino effect on the people around us, and all of those connected to them. We do not have to waste our time nor jump into the ego and try to control other people and the way they live. We must, however, work on raising our vibration, shedding the programming, and learn to live more authentic lives. To rise against a system that is threatening the existence of humanity, we must shed the very parts of us that feed the threat. Connecting with the higher self empowers one to face the darkness within and transform it into the light. We cannot mend the world when we are functioning from a broken space; because we will love, teach, lead, and create from the dark and broken pieces inside. Each layer of trauma, pain, anger and grief that is healed, is another layer of the ego that is dissolved. The more ego you shed, the closer to your true self, you become. If we plan to rise and create a new world of functionality, peace, and unity, then it all must start within.

When we do not have a connection with our spirit, we keep ourselves open to being deceived by the ego and other people in this world. So many individuals get led astray by false prophets, Instagram gurus, religious cults, and wicked leaders because they lack discernment that a connection with their higher self can give. When walking down the path of darkness, the higher self speaks and gives instructions to turn around. That gut feeling or inner whisper was the communication from the inner spirit. It is the higher self that will also send signs in the physical world that will cause one to be in-tune with what is happening around them. God created the spirit, and therefore the spirit is led by God. Feeding the ego is what will sever that spiritual guidance and connection, which will lead to the abandonment of the God that lies within. Once the God within is neglected, then one will seek outwardly to find that spiritual connection. Unfortunately, many ego-driven people are waiting nearby to disguise themselves as the "savior" to lead people further into the darkness. Knowing that we are an extension of the almighty creator, we come to realize how valuable our souls are. Anything or anyone of such great value will be sought out by darkness, to use its power to fulfill the wicked and selfish desires of the enemy. The soul is the wager between good and evil and that is why there are so many distractions created to keep you from going in and finding out why.

Stillness is one of the most powerful techniques used to connect with the higher self. Shutting the noise off of our distractions and closing the eyes will naturally disconnect us from the physical realm and bring us closer to Source. When we fight the silence, we reject our awareness and healing. Meditation is simply being still and letting the soul do the talking. When the mouth is always moving, and the brain is over-analyzing, we are pushing aside Spirit and choosing chaos over peace. There are so many situations that we will find ourselves in that can be dissolved and made right by just allowing the soul to speak and lead. You do not have to run to a temple, an organization or an individual to find your creator. When there are no temples left and no trustworthy people around, there is only one place to find the Divine, and that is within. To trust what you have inside of your vessel, you must build a relationship with your inner spirit.

Building a relationship with the higher self requires the practice of self-love. The relationship with the higher self is just like any other relationship that we seek to pursue with any other individual. When we love someone, we spend time with them, we communicate with them and perform acts of kindness to show that we care. When I tell my clients to practice self-love, they often get baffled and worried because they do not know how to. I, just like many of my clients, was also once very lost and confused when it came to turning the tables of love around. The solution to my confusion was to do for myself what I would do for others, to show them that I cared. Very often, we neglect our own needs, but we rush to save the day for everyone else. One day, I counted how many times I said, "I Love you," to my children and husband, and although they received their fair share of love, I realized I had not said those very words to myself in years. When we do not practice self-love, we are sending a firm intention out that other people's needs, and desires are more important than our own. Anything that is habitually done is a prayer, and one thing about prayer is that it works! So, if you are continuously neglecting yourself, then your prayer is that you wish the self to go away and

THE AWAKENING

make its presence invisible. We always get what we pray for, and we must be careful of what we put out. One cannot develop a relationship with their higher self by also praying it away.

Alone time allows you to shut off everyone else's energy, opinions, and issues and be in tune with everything within. When you spend quality time alone, your spirit voice becomes loud. When the spirit speaks, it will come in the form of a thought, a bright idea, or a burst of inspiration. Your spirit will use its tools to speak to you as well, such as the mind and body. That gut feeling you get when something is not right is a message from your spirit. Those thoughts that seem to come from nowhere that bring clarity is also spirit.

The voice of the spirit speaks with authority, calmness, clarity, and encouragement and is very subtle. The ego speaks with anger, control, fear, and confusion and is very loud. You will find yourself becoming foggy minded and indecisive when battling between the two. To become centered and quiet the ego, set an intention, turn off distractions, and focus all attention towards the heart. Once in the heart space, emotions may come flooding to the surface. Communicating with the higher self is a compelling connection. The moment contact is reached, a sense of closeness and familiarity will be felt. If there is any trouble quieting the mind, try breathwork, it's an excellent technique to quiet and clear the thoughts. The rhythmic breathing techniques in breathwork are used to control the mind and emotions to promote clarity and relaxation.

Asking questions in prayer and meditation is a beautiful way to begin dialect with the higher self as well. Start with only one question per week to develop communication and ease into this new relationship. Just like dating someone new, take it slow and do not rush. Please take notice of how the higher self answers questions posed to it. Patterns that are developed expose the way your spirit communicates. Be mindful that spirit speaks to us through signs as well and will draw your attention towards outside encounters, messages, and objects that carry validation. Always direct your questions to the higher-self or the Creator. Many people experiencing an awakening are eager to communicate with loved ones that have already passed. Jumping ahead will cause a weak foundation in communication with one's spirit. Remember that we are no longer seeking to abandon the self; therefore, discipline must be practiced in order to stay on our path and not wander off.

The most important thing to remember when building this connection with the higher self is to be aware of distractions. There are so many forms of distractions that can interfere with progress. Social media, when not managed properly, will not only waste valuable time, but it also programs the mind and feeds the ego. Negative people, places, and habits also need to be minimized for healthy energy and routines to come through. Entertaining negativity allows the ego to distract one from a higher self-connection. The path of spiritual awakening can be lonely at times, but it is in that space that someone goes within and truly find themselves. Understand that we can also be our own distraction.

Avoiding the truth of who we are and how we show up in the world will stunt our healing and spiritual growth. Working with a coach and/or therapist will help the process of understanding and eliminating the emotional and mental conditions that are lingering and causing harm. Past trauma, abandonment issues, low self-esteem, toxic relationships, and depression are all distractions, that if healed, will go away.

The spirit will be purging during an awakening. Therefore, anything that the spirit views as unhealthy and hindering to the journey will be brought to attention. Follow the guidance of the higher self in order to move through the awakening with grace. There will be challenging times along this path, but the process itself is beyond gratifying. The spirit within will become the closest and most valuable relationship that one will ever experience in any and every lifetime.

THE MIND AWAKENING

The mind of a child is like a sponge, and within the first six years of that child's life, they absorb all information around them without the ability to filter. The way a child's brain works, at such an early age, causes them to be easy targets for conditioning of the mind. Most of us have spent those first years of our lives being taught, trained, and downloaded with information from our parents, family members, childcare providers, and even a handy dandy television. We watched our parents communicate, laugh, cry, and act out their own beliefs in front of us as we sat by absorbing it all. No matter if the people around us were healthy or not, we became a living and breathing extension of who they were. Our minds are very similar to computers; the mind is the hard drive of the vessel. The conscious part of the mind is aware of and living in the present moment. The subconscious mind is the area where information is stored from our past, experiences, and downloads and conditioning. We can only consciously act out what the subconscious mind has received and believes. Therefore, whatever we absorbed has become our reference point in creating the individuals that we are today.

The spirit has a mind of its own, and it works through our intuition. We naturally have a divine knowing that helps us to receive clarity and make better decisions. However, by neglecting the spirit and feeding the ego, we will find ourselves turning off our intuition to follow only the mind. The mind is not a bad thing, but it can be ruthless when it is out of balance and only downloaded with information to serve the ego-self. If the ego is providing all the downloads to the mind then the mind is the slave of its agenda. If the spirit is nourishing the mind then the orders of the spirit are what will be followed.

During this awakening phase, the spirit is purging the mind of the ego's mental conditioning that's un-serving to the soul. Mental programming that contains fears, deception, and spiritual misconceptions cause hindrances that can sabotage one's journey. When the spirit is aligning the mind, it fetches all the harmful conditioning and beliefs and brings it all to the surface for removal. The removal of this unwanted material occurs through healing, truth, awareness, and progressive changes. We cannot be conscious individuals with a mind full of trash. Destructive conditioning also becomes the foundation of what and who we attract in our lives. All the energy within the human vessel is very magnetic. That force naturally draws to it, all that is common. When our mind is out of alignment with our spirit, we will attract people, situations, habits, and more experiences that align with our damaging beliefs. The unhealthy circumstances we draw in, the weaker our will and connection with the divine will become. Fighting the ego is exhausting, for as long as the spirit is starving, one will become weak and succumb to the blows of darkness. The only way to truly fight the ego is to starve it and feed the spirit.

The brain gets programmed through repetition, images, symbols, and emotion. This type of programming is brainwashing. Brainwashing is the use of physiological techniques to control the mind. Everyone that has lived in a society shaped by television, radio, religion, school system, friends and family, have all been brainwashed. Unless one is naked in the jungle and has low to no contact with the outside world, they have been mentally affected by the serpent ego. One bite into the knowledge of the ego can cause one to break away from all things pure and natural. Once fed by the desires of the ego, one can alter not only their path but also the children they bring into this world. Our misaligned beliefs are not just our own, for they are like a contagious plague that reaches from person to person until we are all affected and ill.

The more time taken to research how the mind works, the more transparent the enemy's plan becomes. The enemy's goal with the mind is to program it to fit its agenda. The enemy will draw its subject into its grips through any means necessary in order to remain in control. The mind is a very powerful tool, and whoever controls it becomes the master. The spirit is fighting for the mind to be in alignment with divinity and not a force of evil that seeks destruction.

During this process of awakening, one will feel as though they are losing their mind. The mind is actually in a state of detox, which will naturally cause a reaction of confusion. The loss of the old mind will be grieved and cause one to feel isolated from familiar places, conversations, and people. The spirit during this transition is aligning the mind with its will and plan. Someone experiencing this shift will begin to analyze everything and everyone around them; they will also begin questioning everything that they have previously learned. Children tend to ask a ton of questions when they are between the ages of 3-6 because they are seeking understanding and truth. During the mind awakening phase, one will go back to asking 101 questions in order to unravel the deception and find the truth that was left out. The spirit will be directing the vessel to find truth by sparking interest, manifesting signs, and calling for messengers to deliver a word of hope and guidance. The spirit will be working to take over and guide the vessel down a path of breadcrumbs leading it to its mission/destiny.

As the spirit renovates the mind, it will call for reprogramming to occur. Reprogramming the mind floods the now empty spaces that once contained lies, with truth and knowledge aligned with one's purpose. Just like with a bad habit, once removed, a healthier one must fill the void, or the bad habit will be retrieved. To rewire the mind, use the same brainwashing techniques that were put into place in the destruction of spirit but switch up the content. Repetitively speak to the mind every day with positive words that match one's desires. Affirmations, positive music, literature, motivational speeches are all things that can be used to rewire the mind.

Make sure to absorb positivity as much as possible in all the techniques mentioned, and a change will not only be felt but also seen by others. We must all be on guard at the doorway of our minds, to keep destruction out. An individual that is still asleep consciously will allow any programming to enter as he/she sits idly by without any measures of defense. An awakened individual can feel and sense that specific material will be toxic to them. They, therefore, will block it out and not entertain the darkness trying to enter.

In our society, there are evil powers channeled through unconscious people that control the food, the music, and television. The tools these dark forces use to manipulate, and program people's minds are utilized to keep them asleep, anxious, stressed, unhealthy, and spiritually weak. In order to not regress and activate old programming, one must make changes not to carry in more distractions. Just because one is experiencing an awakening, does not mean they cannot be forced back into sleep mode through their lack of discipline and ignorance.

As the mind continues to get flushed out during the detoxing process, the energy within the vessel will go from a lower frequency to a higher one. Changing one's energy to vibrate higher will allow more positive people, opportunities, and experiences to enter their journey. It is essential to mention that low vibrating thoughts and programming also attract not just low vibrating people but low vibrating spirits. The dark spirits that linger and manipulate the mind are attached to low vibrating individuals, making it harder for the person to rise above low periods in life. Like energy attracts like energy, and being that Spirits are energy, they will naturally cling to other people who match their vibration.

Many individuals suffer from spirits manipulating their minds, and because they are unaware of what is happening, they are misdiagnosed as having mental conditions such as bipolar, Schizophrenia, and other dissociative disorders. Yes, specific imbalances cause medical conditions, such as the ones mentioned. However, there are many people misdiagnosed due to the lack of understanding of spirit and energy. Racing thoughts, excessive mood swings, depression, anxiety, and the inability to focus are also symptoms of spirit manipulation. No matter what the issue, when we are out of alignment, we will welcome disease in all areas of the body, especially the mind.

Years of conditioning will require years of reprogramming in order to be strong enough to silence the ego. There is no need to apply stress to one's journey because of backsliding moments into the ego. As long as the spirit continues to get fed, the ego will naturally get forced into the background. Over time, the change will occur but know that every transformation requires patience and obedience. The mind is an unlimited source of power, and it will get used as a weapon for the ego or a weapon against the ego. Treat the mind as one would a newborn child and protect it from anything or anyone that may cause it harm. When children are first born, they are kept in the home until their immune systems are strong enough to explore the outside world. Just like a newborn child, the mind must be shielded until it is strong enough to face the ego without losing its connection to spirit.

Freeing the mind comes at a price. The abandonment of the old mind requires letting go. Letting go of old habits, toxic relationships, destructive patterns, and even people, is all a part of the transformation process. A part of who we are must die for another part to rise. The evolution of the mind will cause everyone around that is led by the ego to be confused. When an individual is amid conversion, only another awakened one will be able to recognize their state of revision. Stay on the path of light and continue the work and watch how the new mind will be used by spirit to draw in a new tribe, a new life, and new habits.

THE BODY AWAKENING

As the awakening journey progresses, there will be apparent changes that occur within the body during this process. The body begins to adjust, in order for it to move into alignment with the will of the spirit. During this time one may feel a bit out of whack, extra sensitive, inspired to make drastic changes, and more aware of the way the body responds to energy.

The spirit needs a body in order for the will of the spirit to be fulfilled in the physical realm appropriately. The higher self has always remained tethered to the body, but with the ego dominating, the spirit became overshadowed. Spirit has within it, the blueprint of one's purpose and destiny. The spirit communicates with the mind to download its orders, which are then executed by the body. The stronger the connection with the higher self, the more evident one's purpose becomes.

On the other hand, if the ego is in control, then its agenda will be imposed on the mind and carried through by the body. The ego's control causes not only a spiritual disconnection but a physical one as well. When disconnected from the spirit self, the body is then used to fulfill superficial desires as well as establishing unhealthy and dangerous habits that go against one's purpose.

When the ego runs the show, we use our bodies to not only harm ourselves but also other people and the environment. The ego being in control of the body is just like a puppet master pulling all the strings to obtain its own goal. When an individual allows the ego to control the body, they will sacrifice their health, self-respect, relationship with the creator, and their purpose, to fulfill superficial desires. However, when the spirit is in charge, the body is more respected and taken care of to benefit one's journey. The spirit is well aware that the body is a sacred temple that holds a divine and powerful force within. The soul is wise enough to not compromise its connection with its chosen body to fulfill worldly desires.

The moment that spirit awakens, it begins adjusting to its home. When someone decides to rent or purchase a new home, they do a walk-through and determine what needs to be changed or repaired. They may find that the pipes need to be cleared, and they may notice cracks in the foundation that need repairing. Just like a new home, the spirit sees the body as an investment. Spirit goes into full renovation mode during an awakening, molding, and preparing the body to serve its purpose.

While the higher self is doing inventory checks, it will use the body as a tool to trigger various regions to get the mind's attention for repairs. For example, if the Spirit seeks to lessen the body's intake of toxins, it will inspire the mind to become drawn to establishing healthier habits. The goal of the Spirit is to influence the mind to embrace healthier foods and activities that will assist in achieving a more divine state and accomplishing one's purpose. The Spirit desires natural foods, remedies, and other methods of healing that are more in sync with Spirit and created to withstand its journey.

THE AWAKENING

Spirit will also get the mind's attention by increasing symptoms of underlined illnesses and emotions surrounding past traumas to the body so that one becomes aware of issues that need healing. When the soul is more present and active, it will cause its host to be more in-tune to everything internal and external. The result of increased awareness causes one to become more sensitive to their environment, energy, emotions, and food. When this happens, there will be an onset of anxiety, allergies, extreme empathy, and the desire to make changes drastically. The start of the awakening is very profound, but as one begins to adjust by accepting the shift, things will level out.

The spirit in the moment of awakening is rejecting anything and anyone that is negatively affecting its mission. Be mindful that spirit will even use the body to push away sexual partners that are also toxic to one's purpose. Unsettling feelings before and after sex, recurring infections, sensitivity to sperm, and arousal fluids are also signs of spirit rejecting one's partner. The soul is aware of things that the mind may not be willing to embrace, due to its programming and fears, so spirit uses the body to send signals as a warning. Most women are unaware that vaginal dryness is also a form of spirit rejection. When a woman is aroused, signals are sent to the brain to produce fluid to prepare her body for comfortable intercourse. If the chosen partner is not in one's best interest, then spirit many times will intercept the signal from reaching the brain. Many other illnesses and infections can cause all of these symptoms, as well. Therefore, one should seek professional help from their physician to check all bases.

Spirit knows what it needs to complete it's mission and therefore when being led to make changes, go with the flow! Baby step all bodily changes because rushing into everything will cause one to lack the wisdom, strength, and consistency needed to make permanent alterations.

It is through the physical vessel that changes in the physical realm can come to be. For example, the soul's purpose could be to assist in fighting the housing crisis and ending homelessness. It is the physical body that will be present to obtain the education and get downloaded with information to acquire then what is needed for its plans to be executed. It may also be that the physical body must perform the actual work of building homes. If the spirit is called to devise change to the educational system, it will then use the physical body to act out orders and create solutions. Spirit brings forth truth, guidance, inspiration, magic, protection, and connection to reach the goal. However, it is the physical body that completes the orders of the spirit. The body is essential to the journey, and treating it poorly cuts the time short that one has to complete their soul's mission.

To create a clear channel to spirit, we must clear away debris that has accumulated within the vessel from years of mistreatment. Toxins need to be detoxed bit by bit from the body in order for there to be clear and accurate communication with the spirit. When toxins fill the body, these invaders throw off different receptors within the vessel that intercept signals from spirit. When lines of communication are not clear, then accuracy and insight from spirit become threatened. When a person cannot receive guidance from within, they begin to seek outside sources for their spiritual needs and connection. People that lack direct communication with their higher selves unfortunately often come into contact with ill intent individuals looking to manipulate and take advantage of them. The amount of clarity in mind and from the spirit is profound when the body is in a clean and healthy state.

*99% of the human body is made up of six elements: oxygen, carbon, hydrogen, nitrogen, calcium, and phosphorus. Only 0.85% is composed of potassium, sulfur, sodium, chlorine, and magnesium. Eleven of these major elements are necessary for our survival. - Wikipedia

When any chemical is added to an element, it completely changes the composition of that element. We are a direct manifestation and creation of Divinity and designed in the likeness and image of our Creator(s). The chemicals we ingest into our bodies are changing the God molecules and elements that we were born with. The body was not intended to absorb an abundance of chemicals, heavy metals, and toxins that we ingest. The agenda of evil is to keep the spirit silenced, the mind unconscious, and the body weak. The body is a temple, and the job of the enemy is to make it collapse.

This war against humanity has created numerous opportunities for our bodies to be weakened and taken over by evil. With the veil of deception removed, we begin to see how food has been used as a weapon against us. Our eyes are opening to the pharmaceutical companies creating drugs to treat one illness to manifest into another as well as addictions. We are beginning to understand the over-sexualized images and videos that cause us to crave physical pleasures that lead to spirit takeover by parasites we obtain through sex. We see the outrageous number of hysterectomies being done on women that lead to their spiritual portals (wombs) to shut down. We cannot usher in new souls with a mission if the wombs are no longer there to transport them. It is not enough to just wake up, one must stay awake, and this does not happen by engaging in and strengthening the powers that put them to sleep.

SPIRIT

One thing that is and will always be is Spirit. Let us shed our physical bodies now, and back to Spirit, we shall return. Spirit is the only thing connected to our experience that is eternal. Yet, many people still allow fear to keep them from learning and embracing the beauty of its presence in our lives. The truth is, we have never walked this journey alone. Every battle we have fought has been with Spirit right by our side.

The information I give you in this chapter is based on my connection with the spirit realm. I have worked as an Intuitive Medium for the past decade, helping people to heal through spirit communication. I was born with the ability to communicate with Spirit. Still, it wasn't until my awakening that I finally decided to embrace it.

There is a misguided perception that Mediums / Seer's/ Clairvoyants know it all and the truth is, we are always learning and still seeking understanding. By no means do I know everything that has to do with Spirit. I am just one of the individuals that inhabit this Earth with a high level of sensitivity that enables me to see and feel beyond the physical. No one knows everything about Spirit, except our creators. Some things are exposed to specific individuals so that they can be messengers to others. There are also parts of life and the spirit world that are too sacred for our ego selves to enter and understand. I always say, as I grow and learn I shall teach. Your journey with Spirit is your own, and it will be as uniquely customized to fit your experience based on your personality and purpose. In our society, we have a one size fits all mentality regarding Spirit. Although there are similarities, every journey is different. When you are just starting in your awakening, seek guidance, but don't get so wrapped up in your experience looking and sounding the same as everyone else's. If everything were designed to be precisely the same, then there would be no need for your existence.

Spirit; the nonphysical part of a person which is the seat of emotions and character; the soul.

Spirit is proof that all life is eternal and that there is no such thing as death. Spirit brings with it, evidence that life never ceases but merely transitions. Spirit is the soul, the energy, the essence that lives within and out of every physical body. Spirit is our Creators, Ancestors, the Higher-self, the Angels, and those that we have loved, and watched transition. Spirit is nature. Spirit is life. Without the Spirit, there is no us. Minus the Spirit within, we are merely artificial intelligent vessels with no purpose, passion, and connection to divinity. When one fears Spirit, they fear themselves.

THE AWAKENING

The journey of connecting with Spirit brings exceptional benefits to your personal and spiritual life. It is through our connection that we discover more about our spiritual self and our journey ahead. When you are aware that Spirit is all around you, you tend to see with more depth, which by doing so, strengthens your intuition. When you recognize everything and everyone as having a soul inside of them, you allow yourself to see the divinity in others that you typically would glance over. Some of the many benefits that come from having a connection with Spirit are...

- Intuitive Guidance

- Increased Dreams that offer insight and solutions to problems

- A deeper understanding of others

- Heightened Sensitivity Levels

- Warnings from spirit to help you remain safe and protected

- Messages that bring hope and healing

- Connection to one's ancestors to assist in healing generational patterns

- Inspiration and increased creativity

- Knowledge of Spirituality and Self

- Recovering from the grief of a loved one's transition

- Signs and validation from nature and animals to help you on your path

From our creators to ancestors, our daily lives are greatly influenced by spirit. We are fed information, given guidance, and directed by a well-operated system known as our spirit team. Your best interest and the completion of your journey is the goal that your spirit team works to achieve. There may be times when you're entirely off your path, and it is your team that sends signs in hopes to reel you back on course. Your life is to be lived by only you, and therefore your spirit team can not interfere and live it for you. However, they can send some guidance your way when needed. Many spirit teams are mainly composed of one's angels, family members that have transitioned, and ancestors that we have never physically met.

Think of yourself as a small child learning to walk and stumbling around, trying not to fall. Your parents wanted you to achieve those next steps, so they stood by guiding your every move. No matter how much your parents tried to prevent you from falling, they knew that you had to, in order to learn how to walk. Every step with their guidance helped you to get where you are today. Your spiritual journey is symbolic of you learning how to walk, and your spirit team is just like your parents. Waving you down to the finish line, giving you extra room when you need it, and moving hurdles out the way when they can. Your Spirit guides just like your parents have a job to encourage you, give wisdom, and offer suggestions that will keep you focused on the goal.

It is natural for someone experiencing a spiritual awakening to suddenly be more drawn to the spirit world and begin to question and seek answers. It is unnatural to be afraid of the spirit world. Imagine being afraid of your own shadow or the reflection of yourself in the mirror. We have been conditioned to fear what is natural and to embrace what is artificial. You are a spirit, so why would God create you to fear yourself? The reason many people are walking around this earth, feeling disconnected and unaware of their presence, power, and purpose, is because they have abandoned their spirit. When we turn the switch to off, we disconnect from not only ourselves but also the spiritual help that we rightly inherited. You don't need a Quji board or magical tools to hear from spirit, all you have to do is strengthen your soul, and you will naturally see what has gone unseen due to your conditioning.

THE AWAKENING

A natural connection with Spirit occurs when we start doing things like meditating and setting the intention to heal and repair the disconnect from our soul. When we begin taking Healthy Steps to improve our spiritual lives, we automatically place ourselves at a higher frequency. A higher frequency is where the high vibrational Spirits resides, thus making it easier for us to receive important messages and guidance. The law of attraction is always working even if you are not consciously aware of it. Therefore, when we connect to our own Spirit it is natural for us to then become magnets to other spiritual energy that is like our own.

An example of this would be you embracing a healthy and fit lifestyle and deciding to go to the gym and make some changes. You will begin to notice other people in your environment that are going to the gym and embracing the same lifestyle. Until you've set yourself on the frequency of health, you were unable to even see or understand other people that were a part of it. The same goes for Spirit, for you will also attract souls that have like energy to you and your experience. It was your lower frequency and disconnection from Spirit that kept you blinded to its existence and assistance.

Spirit interacts with us through the intentions that we set. When we seek spiritual guidance, Spirit will communicate to us through energetic channels. The active channels that are common for Spirit to use are our spiritual senses, sending messages in nature, dreams, visions, and inspiration. We are all made of energy, and Spirit can manipulate that energy to focus your attention on something or someone that carries the message you're looking to receive. If you were to go outside and ask Spirit a question and sit there for a few minutes, I guarantee you will receive your answer. Spirit may bring by a specific bird that, after doing some research, you may find has traits that align with the question that you posed. You may even notice a picture forming in a cloud or you may become more in-tuned with the way the wind is blowing. Only your interpretation is what counts because it was you that sent out a

THE AWAKENING

signal for help.

Many people believe that Spirit never answers them, but the truth is they are not still and patient enough to see the subtle message in front of their faces. Remember, we have been conditioned for years only to connect and understand our physical attributes and the physical realm. Learning how to read Spirit messages is the same as learning how to speak and understand another language. Again, the more you connect with your own Spirit, the easier it is to understand the language. When you open up to Spirit you open up to the whole spiritual experience. The purpose of Spirit in your life is not to entertain your ego and fulfill your superficial needs; their sole purpose is to help guide you.

If you want to develop your ability to communicate with spirit, keep it simple. There is no need to watch 500 YouTube videos and continue to Google the same thing. All that is needed to hear from spirit is a prayer, some quiet time, and a notebook to write down any feelings, thoughts, or changes that occur. Spirit always answers and if you do not receive an answer it's because you are not listening. Spirit is not human, so the big fireworks display that you are seeking to have when spirit answers are not going to occur. Spirit is subtle and spirit is quiet, just like your soul. When you seek answers and expect to hear a voice giving loud direction, you will be there waiting for a very long time. Spirit is a new thought or random bright idea. The voice of spirit is not in-between your thoughts; spirit is your thought. Our spiritual energy is like a web that connects us all and stems from our Divine Source, our Creator. The human self speaks through words; spirit speaks through energy, and thoughts are energy. We are at all times interconnected, and it is by our intention and focus that allows us to hone into whatever energy or vibration we give our attention.

The spirit world is very much a mystery to all of us. Even though I can

30

communicate with Spirit, there is still a part of that realm that will always be off-limits, as it should. We reside in the physical realm but there are many different layers and levels that the soul will encounter. Living so long in the ego, many people have issues with entitlement and the need to control everything and everyone. No matter what your beliefs are, it would be best if you respected the fact that some things are better left alone. Divine timing and Divine order are in place for a great reason. Spirit comes with a layer of sacredness that's not intended to be in everyone's hands or minds. Your human privilege may work for you in the physical realm. I see too many people obsessing over trying to "know" and master all things of the unknown. It becomes dangerous, attempting to transfer an entitled mindset over to the spiritual realm. Some experiences and knowledge are to be obtained when we venture out of this level of experience. Do not waste time trying to master the spiritual realm when you are still suffering from not mastering your own life. Delving into all things spiritual without patience and real understanding, could cause someone to lose balance and suffer emotionally, mentally, and physically.

As I have mentioned above, you attract the spirits outside of your spirit team that matches the vibration that you project. When you are seeking to connect with other entities and random Spirits, you risk attracting something that can attach itself to you and feed off of your energy. Spirit possession is very real, and it happens more than anyone can imagine.

Most of the time, people are unaware that they are being affected by a spirit because they don't know real spiritual possession when they see it. When someone is possessed by an energy, their demeanor changes, their energy levels drop, and thoughts become obsessive and confusing. Another sign of possession is a lack of memory recall. You will lack specific memories because another spirit was living them out from your body. Possession occurs not only when someone is attempting contact with spirit but mainly from an individual that is not consciously choosing to be present and live in the "now." When we emotionally escape from life, we allow the spirit to wander, leaving an open vessel for another soul to take charge. Being an escape artist alone will invite possession. Now, add in ghost hunting; you will, for sure, allow a random spirit to use your vessel for its own will and desires. Alcohol and drugs are also activities that eject the divine essence from the body and allow dark entities to move in. When you give your spirit reason to leave home, you are basically putting your vessel up for rent.

There is Beauty in spirit, but there is also contrast. Everything in our very existence has a balance. We live in a world with good and kind people, we also live in a world where there are not such good people as well. The spiritual realm is much like our physical one. We must be accountable for our actions regarding spirit. If you are not responsible, then you not only risk harming yourself, but you also tarnish other people's perception of spirit. The kind souls that want to help us are being feared because of ignorance and careless behavior from humans. Not everyone is created to be a messenger for the spiritual realm. A messenger has an assignment to help, and those assigned are carefully chosen. Imagine a carpenter playing the role of a surgeon. Even though the carpenter is skilled at their job, it does not mean they should pick up the scapple and try performing surgery with no training.

Spiritual workers have gotten a bad rap many times because of other people doing work that they were not called to do. The moment something goes wrong, people blame the spirit world. When someone is assigned to do supernatural work, they are equipped with abilities, behaviors, and levels of protection that supports their calling. Seek those that have been called to do that type of work. Pray and meditate for an authentic and naturally called spiritual worker to show themselves to you. Practice patience and an authentic messenger will appear. We must protect the spirit realm from exploitation, lies, and fears that come from our ignorance and other sources. There are kind souls that want to help us make it through by bringing forth protection, understanding, and love. If we aid in tarnishing the image of spirit, we affect others from receiving healing and genuine connection. The spirit realm is sacred and we must treat it as such.

FREQUENCY

What is Frequency? Broadly put, its science, nature, magic, and logic all rolled up in one. Our lives are impacted daily by the energy that we carry and that energy positions us on a specific frequency range. Depending on the frequency that we are on, we can be enjoying most of our lives or suffering miserably. There are many ways to manage our energy so that we are not a victim of circumstance but instead, key creators in the way we show up in our lives and on our spiritual path.

Frequency: the rate at which a vibration occurs that constitutes a wave, either in a material (as in sound waves), or in an electromagnetic field (as in radio waves and light), usually measured per second.

I always compare frequency to a car radio. Imagine turning the dial in search of a radio station that will give you just the type of experience you desire. As your seeking your desired channel, you may come across music that does not interest you, causing you to move on and continue exploring. Once you have found your station, you sit back, relax, and get carried away in the vibration that your chosen music takes you. The channel that you want is set to a specific frequency, and once you're on it, you will receive all the hits that belong to that genre. Similar to the radio analogy, your mindset and actions establish your personal energy. Your energy creates a vibration that sends out an energetic wavelength that places you on a specific frequency. Just like the radio, your frequency will connect you to all things, people, and opportunities on that energetic level. If you do not like what you are experiencing, you don't sit back and try to adjust; you change the station.

Energy does not lie or deceive you, for it is the underlying and foundational part of all things and people. Once you explore and tap into the way energy moves, you can use your knowledge to create better experiences. Understanding your energy output can allow you to more efficiently direct your focus and intentions to reach a higher frequency.

Higher Frequencies carry experiences, encounters, and emotions that align with your deepest desires and passions. Vibrating on a higher frequency opens you up to manifesting things with more ease, smiling more often, healing, and attracting healthier people into your life. Some of the common emotions and experiences that you will encounter when you are on a higher frequency are....

- Love

- Acceptance

- Cheerfulness

- Peace

THE AWAKENING

- Joy

- Enlightenment

- Consciousness

- Mental, Emotional and Spiritual Growth

- Kindness

- Purity

- Compassion

- Deeper Connections with people

- Inspiration

- Motivation

- Honesty

- Authenticity

As you can see, being on a higher frequency is precisely where you want to be. The higher frequency realm is where all of our dreams, desires, and opportunities sit and wait for us. If you desire something, then you have to match the energy of that which you seek. If what you desire is of good energy, but the energy you expel is not, then you're not a vibrational match to the very thing you want. The good stuff is in the Executive Suite, and if we are in the basement looking for our desires, we are not going to find them. To get to the Executive Suite, we must get inside the elevator to rise.

We went over some excellent benefits of higher frequencies, and now it is time to discuss the lower frequencies because naturally, there is a contrast. For many people, staying on a lower frequency appears to be more accessible.

THE AWAKENING

Aside from our daily struggles to emotionally, financially, and physically survive, we also encounter many pitfalls that are out of our control. We live in a society where many times negativity is put on a higher petal stool. From the television, music, politics, and social media, we are bombarded with the dark energy that we deeply wish to escape. Vibrating on a low-frequency sucks, and unfortunately, life happens. Situations will occur that will bring down our energy. If we don't fight to get back up, we will find ourselves adjusting and getting cozy where we are. The longer we stay on a lower frequency, our energy there gets more potent, and no matter how bad it is, we stay there, partly because we don't know how to escape. The worst thing about vibing low is just like vibing high, we attract people, encounters and situations that match the energy that we are now putting out. The Law of Attraction is always working, whether you're playing along or not! Some of the emotions and experiences you will find on a low frequency are......

- Anger

- Fear

- Pride

- Unworthiness

- Shame

- Defeat

- Lack of energy

- Unhealthy Relationships

- Unhealthy habits

- Substance Abuse

THE AWAKENING

- Depression

- Feeling Lost

- Disconnected spiritually

- Unbalanced emotions

- Jealousy

- Judging everyone and everything

- Lack of Creativity

- Suffering

A lack of finances, loss of a loved one, trauma, childhood pain, declining health are just some of the reasons we naturally fall and drop frequencies. Just because you are experiencing a Spiritual Awakening, this does not mean everything will suddenly be brighter and smoother; at times, it's just the opposite. Years of feeding the ego and conforming to society's way of life have allowed many of us to settle on a low frequency and lose our way. We have found comfort in gossiping, judging others, entertaining toxic relationships, filling our minds and bodies with vibrational poison and programming. When our vibration drops, we put ourselves in the position of attracting more dangerous situations. Let me not forget to mention the low vibrating spirits that influence and manipulate the mind. Dark entities love when you drop below the radar because you position yourself in their feeding ground. Low vibrating spirits will feed off of your energy, cause confusion, anger, rage, and deep dark thoughts until there is nothing left of you for them to survive on. Staying on a low vibration makes you the bait that fuels dark energy. Divinity and purity can not survive in such a toxic environment and space. Allowing your space to be filled with such toxicity will cause the soul to wander outside of the vessel, leaving it open for a dark spirit to control.

THE AWAKENING

You don't have to stay in the slums of bad energy, but leaving will require you to make better choices and take a few risks to elevate.

The plan of the enemy becomes very clear when you see what is at risk. Your vessel is up for grabs, and I don't mean to scare you, but it's the truth that I am responsible for sharing. I have witnessed possession, and I have seen it take over a loved one until there was nothing left. Some entities cause rage, promiscuity, addictions, sexual perversion, depression, suicide, and more. So often we dismiss our behaviors as typical actions, just because we are used to them or because many other people suffer from the same things we do. There is NOTHING healthy about walking around bitter, angry, and depressed all day, every day. Just because something is considered normal in society, does not make it okay. The more we feed our egos, the more our frequency will drop. As we feed the ego, the ego feeds evil. We are of God and our divine essence cannot survive and reach its full power by being oppressed and smothered by darkness. When you work to raise your vibration, you are not just simply choosing the spirit over the ego. You are choosing a side of good over evil. Somehow, we have allowed our minds to believe that our toxic behaviors and patterns are okay to settle in. Low vibrations are energetic, contagious diseases, and if we treated it the way we do the flu or a plague, we could stop spreading death amongst each other. "Good Vibes," should be more than just an Instagram slogan; it should be a behavior and mindset that we aggressively strive to achieve.

Reaching a high frequency and maintaining it is critical, but first, you need to look in the mirror and do an accountability check. When you are consciously choosing to tune into a higher frequency, you are taking accountability and changing your actions to move up in rank. I am always stressing the importance of healing our emotions and resolving any trauma that we still hold. When we are carrying around those experiences that caused us great harm, we are harboring the feelings that come along with it. Emotions are energy in motion, meaning active energy that is strong enough to trigger a physical response. Emotions catapult you into a frequency that is the closest vibrational match of the energy you expel. Healing and taking accountability for your attitude, behavior, and actions will release you from the heavy energetic baggage that you carry. You will notice that as you heal from each issue, your programmed ego will lose more and more of its hold, which will make more room for the higher self, naturally causing your frequency to rise. The more you heal, the higher you elevate.

When we do not acknowledge our pain and our actions that are causing us to suffer, we keep ourselves on a frequency of denial. When you ride on the wave of denial, you are opting to have truth, honesty, and growth held back from your experience in all forms. Turning your back from truth trickles down to not allowing those values in your career, relationships, and spirituality. You are responsible for setting the vibrational pace for others to follow.

Speaking of others, let's address low vibrating people. Although you cannot control the general public, you can manage your inner circle. Remember what I stated above "Low vibrations are energetic, contagious diseases." You must pay attention to energy and screen everyone that you bring into your life, home, and heart. Never lose sight of your divinity and its power to spread the healing energy of love into a world of dying and hopeless people. Think of all the influential people, therapists, doctors, counselors, teachers, friendly strangers that spoke life into someone.

Love has the power to talk someone down off a ledge. Love can bring the soul back into position. As an awakened individual, you have the purpose of spreading truth and love so that the world can heal. Your life is of value. The moment you lose sight of that, you will subject yourself to toxic lovers and friends whose egos will seek to disconnect your spiritual light. How many men and women do you know that we're on the right path in life but got knocked all the way down because of the people they let in? As an awakened soul, you cannot afford to risk your rank by getting comfortable in the pits of emotional and energetic hell. Yes, you are here to spread the light and help others, but you are not here to set up camp in the gutter and sign a 2 year lease. Your light shines the best when you are at your best. Teach people how to rise above, share your story of triumph, create platforms to help others but DO NOT allow toxic people to drag you down to their level and feed on you. I will be honest with you...This path of awakening can be lonely at times.

When your vibration increases, you will naturally trigger the people around you that are still vibrating low. Please hear me, your true tribe is coming. Allow the blessing of good people to walk into your life by letting go of those that only seek to drain you and use all of your light for their selfish needs. Walking away at times, allows other people to take accountability for their own life. When they do, they will enable healing. Sometimes we entertain low vibes out of pure comfortability and the fear of losing someone and being alone. However, sticking around is not going to heal anyone, it's only going to enable the negativity to get stronger as you get weaker. You must decide if your life and mission are important enough for you to choose yourself and God's will over your life.

SPIRITUAL SENSES

Most of us have full access to our five physical senses; Seeing, Hearing, Touching, Tasting, and Smelling. What many people fail to realize is that we also have spiritual senses that are constituents to our physical ones. Just as we have physical sight, we have spiritual eyesight. Just as we have the physical hearing, we have the spiritual hearing. Even physical touch, taste, and smell have spiritual counterparts. These senses are abilities that we all possess, not to be confused as spiritual gifts. I will speak later on the topic of spiritual gifts in the upcoming chapter. Spiritual senses come with your spirit self, as your physical senses come with your physical self.

We are living in a time where there is non-stop information being thrown at us. There is an abundance of truth and deception, coming our way daily. The Divine has created us with the spiritual senses to help to discern what is truth verse what is deceptive. Our spiritual insights allow us to hear directly from the Divine, connect with our true self, and to feel the spiritual energy around us. Through our spiritual senses, we can bypass many different layers of deception and also the ego.

In this chapter, you will learn about your spiritual senses and why they are essential and also ways to develop them. We are multidimensional individuals that are evolving through our experiences and healing. As we evolve, we raise our frequency, which exceeds lower vibrations and lower levels of existence. As we continue to climb the ladder to higher frequencies and knowledge, our spirit self becomes more present and prominent. With consistency and dedication, we can develop our senses so they can assist us on our journey.

Our spiritual senses are natural, and although alarming, they are nothing to fear. Having your spiritual tools gives you an extra layer of protection, insight, and guidance during your journey. You are being called to take control of your life, your body, and your soul, and you cannot do this blinded and afraid of your truth.

To help you get more acquainted with your senses, I have composed some information below to assist you. My goal is to keep things super simple and basic. I am aware that there is a struggle with many people to understand the way these senses work. For you to quickly grasp and develop these skills, you must clear your mind of all the complicated instructions and theories that you have already picked up. I have included development exercises for all the senses towards the back of the book in the "Workbook" section. Please take your time and work through them, as there is no rush and rushing will lead to incomplete development. Do not try to develop all your skills at once, for each one will come with its own energy shifts that you must get acquainted with before moving forward to the next. Choosing to develop all of them at once can cause anxiety, confusion, and frustration, due to you not pacing yourself. Follow the guidance of your spirit and allow the natural flow to take place. Your spirit knows precisely what you need and when you need it…... Listen!!

THE AWAKENING

See with the Spirit

Spiritual Sense: Sight, also known as Clairvoyance

Purpose: Used to see beyond the physical realm and outside of the present time.

Location: The mind's eye. The space where you daydream and recall memories

Physical Counterpart: The physical eyes; eyesight. Used to see the present moment and other tangible objects in the physical realm

Symptoms: Daydreaming (Visions), Dreaming with adequate memory recall, Premonitions, Seeing things out the corner of your eye that is not physically there. The ability to see spirit in or even out of your mind's eye and having the skill to visualize and manipulate pictures in the mind's eye are all signs of spiritual sight.

Benefits: The ability to receive spiritual insight and guidance through dreams, visions, and meditation

Blocks: closed-off mindset, lack of trust, unwillingness to see the bigger picture, and the truth surrounding a situation or experience (closed third eye). Unhealthy diet and lifestyle. Drugs and alcohol. Harmful downloads that trigger fear

Development Techniques: Meditation, Visualizing colors and shapes, Daydreaming with Intention, expressing creativity through visual arts such as painting, drawing, building, etc.

Hear with the Spirit

Spiritual Sense: Hearing, also known as Clairaudience

Purpose: To hear from spirit; The higher self, The Divine, and loved ones that are in spirit form. Spiritual ears listen to sounds on other frequencies. Similar to a dog hearing a silent whistle

Location: Inner ear. Voice/message sounds coming from the inside of the body (mind) and sometimes outside. When energy pierces the physical realm, it can be heard audibly

Physical Counterpart: The physical ears. Used to listen to sounds in the physical realm

Symptoms: Ringing in the ears, hearing muffled or loud sounds with no physical source present, fleeting and random thoughts when around other people, anxiety,

Benefits: Spiritual Guidance, musical and artistic inspiration, warnings from spirit, spirit communication.

Blocks: Unhealthy and imbalanced diet and lifestyle. Drugs, alcohol, prescription medication, low vibrations, depression, fearful beliefs, and the inability to quiet oneself and be open to listening. Unhealed trust issues

Development techniques: Meditation, Silent Fasting (Not talking for specified timeframes), Silent time spent in nature, journaling, learning to trust one's self

Feel with the Spirit

Spiritual Sense: Spiritual feeling, also known as Clairsentience

Purpose: Increased intuition, Sensing spirit, being in-tuned with the spiritual self and the physical body, sensing shifts and changes in the environment, nature, people and self, spiritual guidance and protection

Location: All over the body and in any specific region that needs your attention. The stomach and heart areas tend to be more receptive to spiritual energy.

Physical counterpart: The physical body; the gut

Symptoms: drained energy around large groups of people, Intuitive hints about someone before knowing their story, sensing energy shifts in people, environment and within the self, feeling the emotions of others, emotionally sensitive

Benefits: Feeling and sensing the energy around you and within others allows one to filter out deception and uncertainty. Having the ability to validate the presence of spirit. This sense is also instrumental in giving guidance while making decisions. Having the ability to help others, due to having a deep understanding of their emotions. Empathy.

Blocks: Unbalanced emotions, being shut off emotionally, unhealed trauma, improper diet, drugs, alcohol, unhealthy habits and a disconnect with one's body and spirit

Development techniques: Healthy diet and exercise, yoga, meditation, quality time alone, journaling, counseling to connect with one's inner emotions, emotionally opening up more, being present and vulnerable in a safe space

Empaths are very similar to those with a heightened spiritual feeling. Empaths, however, do not just feel others' energy; they absorb it and take it on as their own, which can be very confusing. Empaths are like human chameleons, having the ability to adapt and take on its environment's persona. Empaths are natural healers because of their ability to deeply feel and tap into solutions and methods of healing that may be suitable for the subject they help. Empaths must learn to ground themselves frequently in nature/water, eat healthy diets, and have a healthy amount of alone time to disconnect and recharge their energy. Empath exercise techniques will be in the "Workbook" section.

Knowing with the Spirit

Spiritual Sense: Spiritual Knowing, also known as Claircognizance

Purpose: Accessing the wisdom and guidance from one's higher self

Location: From deep within the heart area

THE AWAKENING

Physical Counterpart: The mind

Symptoms: Analytical (seeking answers deep within but often misguided to use the physical mind), Knowing things without any prior experience of learning, Inner guidance that leads you in the right direction (even if at times, you ignore it), speaking a different or foreign language without prior lessons and even knowing its origin, a deep sense of knowing, very intuitive, know it all persona

Benefits: Inner guidance system, Help making intuitive decisions that benefit your life. Artistic abilities like writing, designing, etc., Problem-solving and a Heightened ability of discernment

Blocks: Mentally shut off, inability to learn, ignoring one's intuitive feelings, drugs, alcohol, improper diet, lack of clarity and peace, mental downloads (brainwashing), social media addictions, too much television, and electronic stimulation

Development Techniques: Meditation, balanced mental health, journaling, writing

Touching with the Spirit

Spiritual Sense: Spiritual Touch, also known as Clairtangency

Purpose: To read more in-depth into someone or something. Picking up on the history and energy of an object or person

Location: The hands

Physical Counterpart: Touch. The hands

Symptoms: Feeling of panic or anxiety in crowded places. Visions or dreams after meeting or touching someone, the ability to locate missing objects, drawn to second-hand stores and other locations with lots of history, inner knowing about a person or object that you have touched, the ability to visualize healing to an ill individual or animal after laying hands over or on them. Always feeling the need to touch things and people

THE AWAKENING

Benefits: Assisting in locating missing objects or people, intuitive guidance, to see through lines of deception and to find answers that you may be seeking

Blocks: Disconnect with the body and spirit, doubt, lack of trusting self, unhealthy lifestyle, drugs, and alcohol

Development techniques: Practice holding an object and writing down any feelings, visions, and knowing that may arise. Let this object be given to you from a friend with no explanation of the story behind it. When finished with the assignment, give your notes to your friend and ask them to validate what you picked up on.

Taste with the Spirit

Spiritual Sense: Spiritual taste, also known as Clairgustance

Purpose: To receive messages from the higher self in communication and/or about spirits experience while in the physical realm. To offer protection from chemicals and poisons in food by triggering a distaste and uneasiness in the mouth and/or gut before even ingesting the food

Location: Inner Mouth and Gut

Physical Counterpart: Mouth

Symptoms: Receiving feelings in the stomach when around certain foods, Mouthwatering or taste of bitterness when in spirit communication, being turned off from certain foods

Benefits: Intuitively choosing better foods to eat, knowing when a feed can be harmful by paying attention to changes in the body when near a specific food (hold a glass of milk and see if you feel slightly bloated or gassy before drinking it), Spirit can impress on you their previous experiences through taste (ex: tasting chocolate cake because Jane's grandma always baked her chocolate cake)

Blocks: Eating disorders and an unhealthy relationship with food, disconnection with the body, lack of self-awareness

Development Techniques: Taste testing, connecting with the body through self-love and awareness, blind taste testing

We have chosen not to be our authentic selves entirely by abandoning the essential connections with our spirit. We are not the body; the body is a tool that either the ego or the soul controls through the mind. We have neglected so many parts of our true selves to be left partial. Of course, life is complicated, for we are not using all the resources that have been given to us to navigate through this human experience. Too many have been pushed in the space of fear to not embrace and use our spiritual abilities. Our worries have caused great suffering and disconnection from our Creators. Spirit is natural. It is only through deceptive downloads from the society that causes us to fear who we are and what we can do. We watch movies about heroes that possess certain powers, and we cheer them on but run from our own. We have been so conditioned to embrace what is not real and leave behind what is. If you believe the Creator is powerful, then why would you ever second guess that its creations are any less. Do not just open your physical eyes, open your spiritual one as well. See what the enemy has been hiding from you. No one or nothing would work so hard to convince you that you are powerless unless they were hiding something sacred that they fear. You are the chosen, and your spiritual abilities are the weapons and tools given to you rightfully by the Divine. Fear will keep you weak. The truth and the acceptance of it will give you back your power. Your spiritual senses, combined with your spiritual gifts (Next Chapter), will make you a force to reckon with. The enemy is not prepared for the power you will unleash in this world.

SPIRITUAL GIFTS

Connecting with your spiritual gift(s) fulfills a deep and natural desire to be a part of something great and helpful to humanity. Everyone has access to their spiritual gifts, but for many, it is not clear what their gift is, and that mystery may be intentional. Spiritual gifts are sometimes hidden away from us until we are ready to receive what comes with embracing them. Just like a rare diamond, one must dig deeper to find something of such high value. The journey of your awakening will undoubtedly take you into the most intimate depths of your spirit. Going so deep inside will reveal your purpose as well as your spiritual gifts. The ego's attachment to greed, power, self, lust, and otherworldly things, can cause a spiritual gift to not surface and/or create its ability to be misused. The ego must be broken down so that you can be made humble and worthy of carrying such a sacred power.

A spiritual gift has divine energy attached to it that is contagious and transformational to the person receiving. Spiritual gifts deliver a very high vibrational energetic charge that sends a spark of light to the soul of its target. For example, think of a car that needs a jump to its battery so that it can startup. When the other vehicle is hooked up to the battery that is drained, the power of the other engine sparks enough juice to get it moving. When you encounter someone with a spiritual gift, the light they carry sparks your light, which helps it to operate and run properly. Now, after you are up and running, you must maintain that light, or it will die back down, just like the battery. With a charged light, you then have a burst of spiritual awareness, inspiration, clarity, healing, and knowledge. Spiritual gifts go beyond just being influenced by Spirit. A spiritual gift is impressed upon someone chosen by the Divine to inject its Divine energy into the world to bring about truth, healing, service, and awareness to others.

The scripture "Many are called, but few are chosen," Matthew 22:14, is what fills my mind when discussing spiritual gifts. Many people want to know what their contribution is and do they even have one. Before I address the variety of spiritual gifts, I first want to speak on who is called to hold such a gift. Many are called to carry spiritual gifts, but only a few have the discipline, the willpower, the persistence, and courage needed to fulfill such a duty. When you hold a spiritual gift, it is not one that you choose; it is one that is selected for you by the Divine. In some form or fashion, you were made aware of your gift from God via a dream, revelation, instruction from a messenger, childhood passions, and through the internal burning desire to help humanity. Although you will go through lessons and challenges to perfect your gift, one of the significant signs that you are gifted is the crowd you attract without effort. The energy attached to someone with a gift reaches out and draws to them, those seeking healing, or service.

What many people do not understand is carrying such a gift requires great sacrifice. Again, you may have been called to hold your gift, but without the discipline, you cannot walk in your calling. Spiritual gifts are valuable, and therefore they must be handed to people that will respect its value and fulfill the Divine calling on their life. To walk the path of your calling, there will be people that you love that you will need to let go of. To walk the way of your calling, there will be sacrifices that you will have to make that will challenge every part of Who You Are. To walk the path of your calling, you may have to experience situations that would cause most people to run. To walk the way of your calling and hold the spiritual gift assigned to you, you may become unrecognizable to even your own mother. If you cannot let go of the little things that hold you back, you will not have the strength to fight the battles that are ahead. We live in a world that is being run by evil, and those evils want to shade out all light and do it with force. It takes a courageous and sometimes delusional individual to stand in the face of evil with nothing but faith and complete their mission. Sometimes that evil will be the face of judgmental people, toxic relationships, poverty, hunger, trauma, temptation, and pain. So, before you go raising your hand asking for your spiritual gifts to be bestowed upon you, ask yourself if you're ready for what comes with it.

Your gift gives you love and light in the darkest of tunnels, and even in your misery, it will pull you out of the shadows. Your spiritual gift is what gives you purpose, so you should have it, but please be responsible for and honor the sacredness of your gift. The Divine does not make mistakes, so you have been chosen and carefully plucked like a rose out of a garden to hold something so powerful.

I want to address the large numbers of individuals online that are hiding behind the gifted title. I have witnessed spiritual healers online and in-person with drug addictions, bordering alcoholism, and treating their vessels as garbage cans. Although people that hold spiritual gifts are not perfect, they are held to a high standard. The energy within and around an individual determines the strength and reach of their gift. When someone is not consciously going against the desires and orders of their spirit, they risk harming the individuals that they attempt to assist. Never seek a teacher or healer without first asking the Divine for assistance. Even if someone is authentic, their energy may not match yours and therefore part of your message and healing will be held back. Do not ever blindly allow someone into your spirit! You must understand that the individuals that want spiritual gifts but do not want to do the work are viewed as easy targets for low vibrating entities. These low vibrating entities see their eagerness and lack of discipline and they will use them to get to you. There are false prophets on every corner and in every social media platform. It is up to you to practice discernment and consult with your spirit and the Divine to be led to the truth.

THE AWAKENING

The awakened must be protective over their soul, for they wear a target. The awakened will do great things, and for that reason, many forces don't want to see that happen.

If you are ready to receive your gift, the first thing you must do is ask. Head to your alter or sit with intention and speak to your Creator about what you desire and why you feel it is time for you to get your gift.

The Creator will answer you back through the signs, visions and inner feelings that you receive. Prior to even asking, start practicing self-love and healing the emotional and mental wounds that you know you carry. Allow Spirit to meet you where you are at by raising your vibration and shedding parts of your ego. Your gift will be bestowed upon you when you are energetically ready. One major thing that holds us back from our gifts is the inability to submit to the Divine. We as humans want to control everything, but in doing so, we forget we were divinely made by our Creator that rules over all man, land and animals.

Humbleness is the key to receiving your gift. You cannot fake being humble because your Creator knows your heart, and if your heart's not ready, then it is not the time for you to receive. Your gift will be given to you when you understand that you will be used to serve others, not control others, not put them in their place, but to serve them. To serve is to be led by the Divine to assist others, even when your ego wants to fight. You will have to learn how to love people that don't love you and fight for people that are sometimes undeserving of your energy. When you are ready for what to use you to help other people, you will not need to seek any longer for your spiritual gift to appear.

I have comprised a list of spiritual gifts for you to view. Some of us are

THE AWAKENING

familiar with religious texts that describe a variety of spiritual gifts. I have included many of them in my list below. However, I want to make clear that we cannot limit the Divine's creation of spiritual gifts. Just because humans see things in a limited capacity, we must be careful not to place those limitations on the Divines creations. We cannot set a number or point to just one reference of spiritual gifts, for God's intelligence is beyond any number and exceeds all information given.

Prophesy	Leadership	Ability to cast away the darkness	Empathy
Power of the tongue/Speaking tongues	Service	Faith/Increased Manifesting ability	Encouragement
Discerning spirit Mediumship	Intercession	Spiritual Healing	Telepathy
Laying of hands	Teaching	Channeling	Music

Counseling	Herbal Healers (healing others with nature)	Astrology	Innovation
Performing Miracles	Remote Viewing	Warrior (supernatural strength)	Priest/Priestess

There are, of course, many more gifts to list. Not to mention have never been recognized as a gift. Understand that any talent that you possess can be used as a gift to help shape and heal Humanity. If you are a Baker, then use your talent as a gift by using ingredients that raise the vibration of your clientele; instead of getting them hooked on deadly sugars. A Hairstylist can use their ability as a gift to feed encouragement, motivation, and inspiration to their client, raising their vibration to consciousness. An Architect can use their talent as a gift by building homes that house the poor and bring solutions to the housing crisis. A Teacher can use their passion to spread conscious knowledge to their students instead of indoctrinating them with more lies and conditioning. If you are a musician you can use your gift to speak life, knowledge and consciousness to your listeners instead of dropping low vibrational messages that hold them back.

Talents are naturally skilled passions, and when used to feed the spirit and raise the consciousness of others, it transfers into a gift. Your spirit and its true and pure intentions to serve others is what releases the supernatural power that converts its purpose. Your spiritual awakening is not just for you; it is also for the people that you reach and that you touch. You have light within you, so your gift is the ability to use any talent that you have or accumulate to drive that light into others.

For everyone walking in their gift and seeking to obtain their gift, the end goal is the same. Use the light you have to overshadow the darkness. Your gift is your weapon against the enemy and the destructive systems that were created to oppress millions of people. A gift is to be given away, not hoarded in a backroom guarded by our fears and insecurities. The world needs you, your talents, your love, and your passion for serving. Outsiders may not understand the awakened and what they are here to do, and it is not our job to explain. It is our job to roll up our sleeves and get the mission done.

DREAMS & SYMBOLS

My favorite time of the day is when I climb into bed, with my journal nearby, anticipating the adventure that will unfold when I close my eyes. The dream world is where we are limitless, free, and defying all sense of time. Some people don't remember their dreams, and others dismiss them as some mental jambalaya that occurs when they sleep. Dreams carry messages, hope, and hidden truths. When you dream, your spirit seeks what it needs and gets restored with energy and wisdom to continue its journey. In this chapter, I will go over the benefits of dreams, the language of our spirit, and the messages we receive in the dream world. There is a way to peer into your subconscious mind, communicate with your soul, and receive guidance all while you sleep. Dreams are not leftover thoughts or empty events floating around your head. Dreams are sacred, and when you learn to decode them, you will understand the language of the spirit.

Dreams are a spiritual vehicle that allows you to communicate and receive insight from the spirit world, spaces, and places where time does not exist. Dreams will enable you to process healing by seeing deep into your subconscious mind where programming may be causing some interference. When you dream, your spirit wonders and travels to where it needs to be to bring back to you, valuable information and insight. When the world feels as though it is falling apart and communication is lost, dreams will help you find your way and navigate through the chaos. Our ancestors relied on their dreams to warn them of danger, inform them of what foods were good and not good to eat, and to give them hope when all faith appeared to be lost. Many of us still have family members that receive prophetic dreams, and whenever they speak up, we know to listen. In my family, when someone had a dream, we stopped everything and tuned in, as though the Divine descended from the heavens with a special message.

I have worked with many people that believe they do not dream. Research shows that everyone dreams even those that don't remember. Not only does everyone dream, but they dream a few times in one cycle. So why do some people remember their dreams and others don't? Well, firstly, many of our dreams reveal memories of the past that we have not yet healed. Our spirit pushes what we need to repair to the surface, and many times, these issues appear during our dream state. If our memories are very traumatic, our minds' defense mechanism will make attempts to block it, thus causing us not to remember details. In situations regarding trauma and blocks, I suggest seeking a therapist and also trying hypnosis to assist you in memory recall and to help your healing process. Once the blocks begin to move, your dreams will start to open up.

Another thing that causes us not to have much dream recall is our lack of sleep and unhealthy sleeping patterns. We are hardwired to be on the go from the moment we wake up to the time we hit our beds, we pass out from exhaustion. When you are not getting adequate sleep, you are going to have trouble remembering your dreams. A lack of sleep is not healthy, and even though your spirit is jumping around in the spirit realm, your body is struggling to get enough rest. A further reason that people don't remember their dreams are that they don't take enough time in the morning to recall them.

The moment the alarm clock goes off, you jump out of bed or open your eyes and start thinking about the day that you don't want to complete. To recall your dreams, you must lay there for a moment, and before you even get out of bed, take a few deep breaths and write down the smallest thing that you call to mind. Remembering your dreams requires consistency and intention. If you consistently write the smallest details that you can recall, you are setting a firm intention that you desire to bring forth events from your dreams. Documenting your dreams on paper and keeping track of the symbols is what I call a "Dream Journal." Remember, that intention is very strong and powerful. With enough sleep, firm intention, and a journal, your dreams will build from just a glimpse of a whole story that you will recall.

Deja Vu is also the recall of what you experienced in your dream state. That is why when you have Deja Vu; you feel as though you have already been there, and you have, except it was in the dream world.

One of the things that I love about dreaming is learning the language that the Spirit speaks. Symbols are people, events, images, colors, etc. that are used by Spirit to relay a message. When Spirit speaks to us, it's the same as someone that speaks in a different language than you are unfamiliar with. In order for that person to get a message across to you, you may have to use pen and paper or hand motions for them to understand you more clearly. In your dream state, Spirit uses images that I call symbols to communicate with you. For example, many are familiar with the fish symbol. In my family if someone dreamt of a fish that meant somebody is pregnant. One of my personal symbols that appear often in my dreams is water. When I see someone go into the water and come back up, that means they are about to go through a significant transformational in their life.

On the other hand, if someone goes into the water in my dream and does not come back up, that means they will be transitioning into the spirit world soon. I know the meaning of my symbols because I write down my dreams every night. Although it may sound tedious, if you document your dreams, you will learn the language that Spirit speaks. Just like any language, you must study it repeatedly if you desire to speak it fluently. Not all symbols read the same for everyone, which is why documenting your dreams are important and better than rushing to Google every time something appears. Many of you are having prophetic dreams, and you have no idea because there is a lack of record to go back and reference.

As you develop a dream dictionary, you will notice that the symbols you receive will begin to appear in the physical realm in conjunction with other signs. In this dimension, we have developed a language that is way more complex and filled with many hidden messages and spells. In the spirit world, messages are more childlike and simpler. It does take time to shed our complexity to understand spirit, so be patient.

If you are a spiritual practitioner, your symbols will also appear when you are performing any healing work for other people. You will notice that your symbols will appear in your mind's eye when working on a client. Knowing the meaning of those symbols helps you to tap into your client's life and better serve them.

Dreams reveal all types of messages that can help us in our lives, including warnings that can keep us away from danger and ill-intended people. I don't know about you, but I have dated some supreme little demons that wanted to steal my light and sanity. People are tricky, and you can't avoid running into low vibing individuals, but you can keep a safe distance with the help of your dreams. Every time I would meet someone, my dreams would reveal who they were on day one. The only reason I made it to day twenty is because I would second guess what was shown to me or create some excuse to move forward with that person. Yes, there will be times that you won't see danger coming and partly due to the lessons these people carry for you to learn. Some things we have to experience, for our personal growth. However, some encounters are avoidable, and the warning of who you are dealing with will show up in your dreams if you are open to it.

My dreams were always truthful, and if I had listened, I could have saved myself so much heartache. Still, a person often does not want to see the truth; sometimes, people want to drift in the blissful state of illusion. Your awakening journey is all about opening up to the truth, and the more open to it that you are, the more you will see.

We are consumed with deception from our governments, health care systems, media, and more, and until we strengthen those spiritual connections, we risk falling victim. Allow spirit to help guide you so that you do not have to endure extra trials of pain and suffering. You are a spirit before anything else, and you did not come to this earth alone. Your spirit team wants to help, but you also need to make some changes, so it's easier for them to communicate with you and develop a connection through language.

Staying glued to our phones, scrolling through social media obsessively, eating the wrong foods; will begin to deteriorate our spiritual connection. In doing so, we limit the information that can be sent to us from spirit in our dream state. I and so many others, have been warned about food shortages, harmful medications, upcoming wars, and these things were not sent to inflict fear, they were sent to us so we could have time to prepare and adjust. The society built around us is full of corruption, cover-ups, and trickery. Without our dreams that bring truth and warnings, we would have limited ways to protect ourselves.

THE AWAKENING

Our ancestors knew to look towards nature, messages from spirit, and their sacred dreams for divine guidance in everything that they did. Our elders knew that if they asked in prayer for help, guidance, and wisdom, that signs in their everyday lives would begin to appear, to show them their way. We lost our connection to the land, spirit, and ourselves when we stopped relying on nature and spirit and adopted to put our faith and trust into these ego-driven systems. I do not just ask of you, but I warn you to develop a relationship with spirit in your dreams, waking life, and meditations. Create healthier habits so that your body gets adequate rest to heal. We are on the brink of a significant transformation in our societies. However, with the change, there will be a period of destruction. This is not the time for you to be blinded, for what is coming requires you to see and trust in truth and to do so, you must strengthen all of your spiritual connections.

SPIRITUAL MAINTENCE

We cleanse our homes to remove germs and mess that we've accumulated, and in doing so, we make our spaces cozy and inviting. When we clean our homes, we feel good about our area. We are not just moving physical objects around; we are also moving about the energetic debris that has gathered. If not now, you will soon see that as you continue to grow spiritually, you become more sensitive. The more sensitive you become, the more you're able to pick up on energetic debris that tends to linger in your home. Without proper cleansing to your environment, unwanted energies will remain and hide behind your physical clutter. Even though you may not see all the energetic mess lingering, it will still trigger you to feel uneasy and often irritated. Spiritual cleansing has been around for centuries and is something that our ancestors have passed down to us in various ways. Without proper and frequent cleaning habits, your thoughts, your energy levels, your mood, and your ability to manifest are at risk. There are incredible benefits to keeping your home spiritually cleansed, and there is also a downside to not doing so at all.

Spiritual cleansing is using techniques and intention to clear away any stale and low vibrating energy from your physical environment and person. Energy from arguments, illnesses, visitors, and lingering spirits become trapped in our homes. Even though situations may change and people leave, the residue lingers and affects those dwelling in that space, often without their knowledge. Moving into a new home and office space without thoroughly cleansing is like wearing someone else's dirty underwear.....ewww! If not gross enough for you, just think of all the energetic bacteria that will then become your problem. The people that were in the space before you may have gone through bankruptcies, divorce, addictions, depression, etc. When you and your family or business take over the area, everyone there now becomes a victim to what energy is remaining. Everyone has their own set of spirits that accompany them and depending on their vibration; they may have some dark entities attached. For this reason, be careful of who you invite into your home, you would hate for something that was attached to a visitor to linger and begin to affect you and your family. I cannot stress enough how important it is to practice spiritual methods of cleansing and protection.

As an individual that is now consciously awakened, you must take responsibility for the energy around you and the energy that you bring to the table. Have you ever heard the statement, "Next to cleanliness is Godliness?" To understand this phrase, you must know how energy works. When you live in filth and clutter, you attract low vibrating energies and spirits that love to hide and feed off of your energy. When your home is clean, you feel comfortable, relaxed, and at peace. In a clean home, your mind is more clear due to less energetic debris taking up the space that you are in. When your house is messy, you feel irritated, bothered, off-balance, and even ungrounded, which leads to drops in your frequency. When your frequency is low, your connection to high vibrating spirit and the Divine becomes compromised.

I'm well aware that there are hundreds of ways to cleanse and protect your home, but I am going to list just a few of my favorites and trust that you will do some research for more. Listed below are techniques that I perform sometimes weekly, monthly or when changes occur in my home or business. Try out what techniques speak to you, and don't be afraid to create your cleansing rituals. Invite God, your Angels and Ancestors to walk with and support you during your routine. Your spirit team will help to guide you to locations that need more attention, as well as helping to push unwanted energy out.

Smudging with Sage:

Although sage has grown in popularity over the years, Native American cultures have been using it for centuries. The ritual of burning white sage and other dried herbs have been used for spiritual purposes such as spiritual clearings, preparation for different rituals, protection from enemies, vision quest, communication with the ancestors, and many more other sacred practices. Additional herbs sometimes mixed with sage is sweetgrass, cedar, lavender, and copal resin, which is used for cleansing and protection. Sage as an herb is an air purifier. It is believed to have antimicrobial properties that help kill fungi and bacteria. The same way sage can purify and bring nutrients to your body; it can do the same to your space energetically.

Burning sage throughout your home, office, and the car is like a big eraser for negativity and low vibrating energies. When smudging your home or space with sage, first set your intention and say a prayer that aligns with your reason for performing this ritual. After placing your intention, open all the windows in the space that you choose to sage so that the toxic energy has a way out. Go from room to room, reciting your prayer or affirmation while moving the sage in a swaying motion. Make sure to open up closets and get in the corners of the room were energy hides and accumulates. Now, I want to make note that you should clean your home before smudging. If you're going to do a quick sage and your house is semi-clean, then okay. Just note that smudging filth is counteractive.

The most important thing when it comes to Sage and any other spiritual cleansing technique is setting an intention. Intention is very strong and powerful, so do not skip that step. I burn my sage in an Abalone shell and use a feather to circulate the smoke. If you don't have a shell, you can use any fire-safe bowl that you have handy. Before smudging the home, use your sage on yourself to clear your aura and raise your vibration for better results.

Palo Santo:

Spanish for Holy wood, Palo Santo, is a mystical tree grown on the coast of South America. Palo Santo is used for energetic cleansing and healing. You will love the smell and the high vibration that comes with burning Palo Santo. You can use this wood to prepare for other sacred rituals, add to your sage for cleansing, and it's excellent for meditation. Palo Santo is recommended for also grounding your energy and aiding in physical healing. This holy wood is used medicinally as well to help strengthen the immune system, relieve common colds, flu symptoms, and help with easing anxiety. Use your Palo Santo in the same way you would your sage when clearing your home or space. A little tip is to shave the wood onto your sage and burn it altogether.

Incense:

Used for aromatherapy, meditation, and other sacred ceremonies, incense is an easy and quick mood lifter. The aroma of incense will lift your spirit and raise the vibrations of your space. Incense has been used for rituals, magic, offerings to spirit, energy clearings, and purification since ancient times. What I love about incense is that there are so many different oils and blends you can choose from. As with any other ritual, setting your intention will direct the energy you are looking to bring in. Burning incense during meditation and even when preparing for bed, will calm your mind so that you can better relax.

Sound Therapy:

Everything is energy! Like we discussed in the chapter "Frequency," our energy gives off a vibration that sets us on a specific frequency. The frequency

THE AWAKENING

of our home can be affected positively through sound therapy. Sound therapy is used to lower blood pressure, lift your mood, lower anxiety, sleeping disorders, and as a tool for pain management. Music and the sounds of nature are naturally healing. Music, Singing bowls, Chimes, Drumming, Binaural beats, Natural sounds, Instrumental can all be used to set a specific tone and vibe in your home and office. Music can create a mood of peace, prosperity, and happiness. Sound therapy is one of the fastest ways to raise the vibrations of your space. I personally set my intention, open the windows, and go around my home playing or creating music until I feel the mood is set.

Floor Washes:

Now, this is my favorite "Good JuJu ritual!" One of my absolute favorite things to do when I am venturing into a new season is to wash my floors with good intentions. Floor washes are old school and done by many that practice Santeria, conjure hoodoo, and other African spiritual beliefs. We all have that grandma that seemed to mop her floor using specific motions while humming to the loud music playing in the background. Cleaning the floor may have looked like a chore, but that's only because many of us were not aware of the deep-rooted magic and cultural traditions it was based in.

If you are looking to attract money, cleanse negativity out your house, prepare for the new year and bring in health and prosperity, then floor washes may be your thing. When you are performing the floor wash you first as with anything else want to set an intention. Depending on what your intention is you will then add specific herbs and oils to your water that you will cleanse your home top to bottom with. Always start from the back of the house and work your way to the front. Even if you have carpet, you are going to mop that as well (Of course have the mop a little damp). Some of my "go-to" ingredients for floor washes are

- Van Van: A blend of Asian grass extracts, used to cleanse and purify

- Florida Water: Protection, Ancestral connection and cleansing away bad juju

- Rose Water with Jasmine: Good for vibrations of Love

- Holy Water or Blessed Rain Water: Cleansing, Protection, and Peace

- Salt Water with Frankincense and a sprinkle of brick dust: Used for heavy cleansing and protection

- Cinnamon & Vanilla: Used for protection, prosperity, luck, and Love

After mopping your home, you can dispose of the dirty water away from your property line.

I suggest adding in some sound therapy while you do your floor wash and remember to thank the Ancestors while performing your ritual. Sacred rituals are deeply rooted in culture, so if you neglect sending thanks and appreciation to those ancestors, you weaken the power of your intention. Many of the rituals shared around the world today come from indigenous tribes that have been pushed to the background while their rituals have been appropriated. Don't let your ignorance get you in a pot of hot water with the Ancestors…...Pay your respects!!

Florida Water:

This fantastic product was created to be a cologne. Due to Santeria and Voodoo practices, it has grown in popularity. It is used by many people to cleanse their homes and office space. You can add Florida water into your floor washes as a base to clean. I like to carry a small spray bottle with Florida water so that I can have some protection with me wherever I go. If Sage is like a karate student that earned his black belt, Florida water is like six ninjas!

Cleaning:

Get out the old broom and mop and turn on some early school music and start to clean your house. Cleaning is not only an excellent way to cleanse out negativity, but it should be the foundation of any other spiritual cleansing ritual that you use. It is essential to keep a clean home so that your mind and energy remain clear. All of our homes get messy from time to time because of our busy schedules or simply because we don't want to clean all day. Still, your house should not be messy for over a couple of days unless you are sick. Once your better, get up and sweep all that low vibing energy out the front door! When you clean away physical germs, you are clearing away spiritual bacteria, so grab a bucket and raise your vibes.

Oil:

Essential oils all bring forth their properties such as frankincense for cleansing, Sage for purifying, rosemary for stimulating, etc. Find the right oils for you that support your goals. Pray over your oil, which is setting an intention into the oil. Use your blend to spread over door frames in your house to keep unwanted energy from entering. Another good tip is to add your chosen oil to a spray bottle with clear alcohol and spray your intentions throughout your home, car, and office.

Spiritual Baths:

This is like hitting reset on your body, mind, and spirit. Spiritual baths cleanse your energy and set some good intentions to remove or to add something to your person. It is not just our homes or objects that get covered in spiritual goop; we also have unwanted energies sticking to our aura. As energy accumulates on our person, our moods begin to suffer, and we will start to attract other people and experiences to us that match what has attached itself. Spiritual bathing is the most effective way to rid your body and mind from debris. What I love about spiritual baths is that there are so many rituals with set intentions that can help you in almost every area of your life. When I think of people getting baptized, I automatically think of it as a powerful spiritual bath connecting you to the Divine. There are so many rituals passed down in literature that can assist you in making the perfect bath for your needs. In my personal and professional opinion, this ritual is ideal for empaths to thoroughly cleanse their energy after spending a lot of time around people. If you also work in providing any therapy and spiritual healing work to others or take frequent trips to Wal-Mart... I highly suggest weekly spiritual baths.

Detoxing:

What you do in the physical will be done in the spiritual. Once a month, I do a detox to perform a cleansing on the inside of my body as well. We cannot just take care of the outside and neglect the inside because what is happening within is projected outwardly. Detoxing your body of unnecessary toxins, harsh metals, and environmental debris that we pick up from pollution will allow you to vibrate on a higher frequency. Those physical parasites that you obtain through food and water also have a plan to break you physically down. Proper diet and regular detoxing will stop the growth of parasites and other diseases that attack your physical vessel and take you out of alignment.

Sweat Lodge Ceremonies:

Many Eastern cultures and Native Americans use sweat lodges for religious ceremonies. Sweat lodge ceremonies consist of prayer, chanting, meditation, and cleansing of your mind, body, and spirit all at once. Sweat lodge ceremonies are very intense, but the feeling will leave you lighter than a feather. Attending a sweat lodge ceremony is comparable to someone pressing a reset button that clears you from your crown chakra down to your root. I highly suggest a yearly sweat lodge ceremony for anyone that is practicing any healing work and doing spiritual readings.

Please be careful when choosing a ceremony to attend and make sure that it is performed by someone that is a professional and that is connected to

Sacred rituals through their ancestral

lineage. There are so many people that profit off of using ancient techniques for greed and popularity, and they are watering down the powerful ancestral connection that occurs through these rituals. Some cultures are deeper rooted in sacred ceremonies, and I personally and spiritually believe those are the individuals you should be going to. If you want African/Native/Hispanic spiritual rituals performed, then go to someone not only deriving from that culture, but that has practiced the ways of their ancestors. This is not to exclude anyone else but merely to inform you of the truth, to help you have an authentic healing experience. Spiritual Healers are chosen to perform sacred rituals passed down from their ancestors. The blood of a spiritual healer connects them to the wisdom, power, protection, and insight of their ancestors in spirit. So when the chosen healer is helping someone, it is their ancestors that surround them and assist in the rituals being performed.

People Detoxing:

Don't knock it until you try it! Do you have mood swings? Are you not feeling like yourself? Experiencing paranoia and negative thoughts? Before you start jumping to other theories, think about the people you surround yourself with. We can love our friends and family to the end of the world but that does not mean that their energy can't be toxic to your journey. Everyone in this world is going through something right now and everyone has their own set of insecurities and fears. When you are consistently around a group of people, you absorb not just their good qualities but also the negative ones. Detoxing yourself from people by not engaging for a few days will allow your energy to be cleared of their negativity and issues. It is also vital for you to practice energy detachment daily so that you are not absorbing and carrying around everyone's energy as though it is your own. Some quick tips to practice energy detachment are cleaning your aura on a regular basis with sage, take weekly spiritual baths and recite affirmations like this one...... "I wish to detach myself from (Name) energy." This information is beneficial to get you through the week.

THE AWAKENING

Empaths are basically like those sticky traps for flies, so detoxing and detachment rituals should be regular. Take a weekend where you do not interact or communicate with anyone. Spend some quality alone time with yourself and set an intention to remove other people's energy and to disconnect it from your person. Run a spiritual bath and get in tune with your emotions, feelings, and thoughts throughout this time. The moment you go back into the world and step outside of your bubble, you will quickly notice the shift in your energy. The detox is not to seclude yourself from the world in an unhealthy way, but rather a time for you to recharge and get clear about your thoughts and feelings. Participating in a people detox once a month is for your spiritual, mental, and physical health. People detoxes are also very useful when you are trying to connect with your intuition. Often you may feel as though you can't hear your intuition, but it's really because you have so much coming at you from other people. When you silenced the world around you, your spirit gets louder.

THE PROPHECY

After 40 days of Fasting and prayer, I asked spirit to speak through me and to deliver a message for everyone that would read this book, myself included. This channeled message is a form of automatic writing.

There is no time coming. The time is now. Your heart seeks for the end of suffering, an end of what you see and feel does not belong. The spirit knows the cycle and rhythms of the Divine, but the ego lacks understanding. What you see as oppression is the Divine strengthening you for battle. What you see as torture is the Divine sharpening your spirit. No change will come if you have convinced yourself that all things are good. War is not pretty but at times necessary. Your oppressors are powerful only because you see yourself as weak. You do not get to love and light without destruction. The flowers don't bloom until the season of death passes. How long will you extend this season? When will you stand and fight back? You have the tools to be warriors, and yet you use these tools for excuses to be weak. The light cannot shine on the path of victory if it hides behind the enemy.

If you genuinely sought a connection with the creator, you would see and feel your power. Reciting empty prayers and dressing for meetings in broken temples does not constitute a relationship with the creator. If the creator had a phone, would you call? What would you say? Would you be proud to speak of the way you perform and degrade yourself when you think you are unseen? How about your mission? Are you any closer to bringing change into this world, or have you gotten distracted with all the pretty deception laid before you by the enemy?

Those that carry the light, where have you gone? Where are your lanterns that are supposed to light the path for those sent to follow? Where are the signs that you have destroyed systems and temples of the enemy? You should have the rubble of their buildings underneath your footsteps. Why are your sisters and brothers starving? Why are the children being taught to fight on the side of evil? Where are those that carry the light, are they no longer alive? Divinity is in this world. Divinity is within, but you have allowed the ego to shut down the works of God and work for the likes of the darkness. Do not pray for God to show up. God has shown up. God is inside the belly; you feed poison. God is inside the body that you hate and filled with chemicals to impress the enemy. God is inside the womb that you corrupt. God is inside of the mind you feed filth. God is in the lungs that you use to breathe death. God is inside of the men that you degrade. God is inside the women that you strike. God is inside the child you abandoned. Why do you cry out for God but work to destroy its presence when it shows up?

Where is your courage? Did you lose sight of your limited time on earth? Do you believe you will have a vessel forever, even though truth shows up every season to prove otherwise? The enemy is increasing in numbers because you're too busy looking through someone else's window. You have filled your time with distractions, complaining, and things that do not matter. Your enemy is powerful because you fall for the traps set before you. You have inherited the land, but yet you choose not to use it. Food lays at your feet, but you decide to slave for coins to buy what is not free. Do you not know how soil works? Water falls from the sky so that you may fill your cups,

THE AWAKENING

but you choose to slave for bottles that pollute your land. Trees were created to give you fresh air, but you choose to cut them down and suffocate. Do you not see that you are sick? Do you not see the error of your ways?

The enemy is powerful because you practice division. God gave colors for creativity, and yet you use them as a source of hate. Separation due to the amount of paper in your pocket makes no sense. Money is paper, and yet you have been easily convinced it does not grow on trees. You should separate good from evil, not the paper from paper. Do you not see the ill mind behind this? You separate yourselves because of religion. God did not create religion. Any religion that carries a date of origin was never here at the beginning of creation. Creation has no age. Let nature be your religion. Let Love be your bible. You pray and worship to man, and your ways of life validate that. You give power to the enemy, and that is why it roams with strength. You fear truth and sleep with lies but somehow are left confused with the lack of honesty in the world.

You cry for change when you are the one chosen to bring it.

Know that God is inside. When you accept this truth, things will change. When you feel the warrior inside, you will be empowered to fight this war and win. When you know who you are, you will respect others because they also carry another piece of God within them. When you know who you are, you will stop poisoning your bodies. When you know who you are, you will break free from oppression. When you know who you are, you will join forces with one another and knock the enemy off its throne.

You have come to this place many times before. Nothing here is new. This has all happened in another lifetime. Chance after chance to get it right, and yet you still choose the path of darkness. To see the light, you must break the

THE AWAKENING

pattern, or the cycle will repeat. This is the bad dream where you keep running from the boogeyman. Now is the time you stop and face what keeps chasing you. Do not look for someone to save you; you must rescue yourself. The division does not work. Feeding the system leaves you weak. Following the blind will leave you lost.

Until you rise, you will be a victim of what the enemy has built. You will drown in the sea of sorrow. You will burn in the fires set by man. You will cry out in hunger from the famine that the enemy has set in place to control you. There is no end down the path of darkness. If you choose to see peace, you must create it.

The power you seek to bring change is within. When you ignite your strength, all things will open to a new phase. What will be destroyed will allow growth. Don't fear destruction, for it brings a new beginning. Celebrate when you see the system of the enemy failing and use it as a doorway to create something new. There is no more time left. The time of destruction that has been prophesied is now. Those that choose to be buried under the bricks of the enemy leave them be. Focus on your spirit. Feed the Spirit, starve the ego. Protect your prophets, healers, and warriors, for they will lead, heal and fight for the light. Keep the children safe. Lead simple lives, for the earth will soon be reset back to its original state. She is on her last trimester, and when the water breaks, all will be wiped out as new life is ushered in. If you don't learn the ways of the land, leave your egos behind, and return to nature, you will not survive the next wave that will hit. What is soon to come is more potent than any virus, hotter than any fire, and more powerful than any earthquake ever felt. Those that carry the light will lead a new generation to tend to the land and the God within. Do not lead them astray for if so, the pattern will repeat. We must break the pattern and to do so, we must start within.

This is the prophecy. Peace be with you. - Rhoni "Genesis" Le

THE WORKBOOK

Creating a Sacred Space:

A Sacred Space is a place that you create for all your spiritual needs, somewhat like your private temple at home. This is the place where you will reflect, meditate, journal, connect with spirit, and develop your one-on-one connection with the Divine. Sacred spaces are known to be physical temples that are also seen and recognized in the spiritual realm. This is the space where your ancestors, your higher self, and the Divine will connect with you.

Step 1: Locate your space. Make sure its a comfortable and private area. Your sacred space could be in your closet, a corner of the room, by a window, etc.

Step 2: Clean & Clear your space. Once you have cleaned your area thoroughly, smudge it, and set your intentions.

Step 3: Decorate your space. Add a small table, your journal, a plant, a candle, and a glass of water. The journal is to write what's in your heart and whatever messages you receive in meditation. A plant represents life and the creator. The candle once lit means you are ready to connect to your spirit self (Like your "on" button). The glass of water also represents life. Water is a conduit for spirit energy, helping to usher in clear messages. Make sure to change your water frequently. You can add pictures of yourself, ancestors, or inspiration.

Step 4: Stand over your space with your hands extended out and recite a prayer or declaration over your area. Close your eyes and visualize all the healing, connection, and spiritual growth that will happen in your space. Before opening your eyes, say out loud, " And so I let it be." Use your area often, for the more work you do, the more the healing energy around your space will grow.

Opening Connection with the Higher Self (Meditation):

This meditation is for connecting with your Higher Self and begin to develop a genuine relationship that will assist you on your journey. The higher self is the spirit that lives within your body. The higher self is an extension and direct connection with the Divine that will give you guidance, protection, and wisdom. Make sure that you have no distractions during this exercise. As the bond grows, you could do this in the middle of a warzone and be able to focus, but during the learning phase, keep things peaceful.

Step 1: Go into your sacred space. Make sure to have a journal and pen right next to you and open it to a clear page. Set your intention to connect with your Higher Self and light a candle to begin the meditation.

Step 2: Take a few moments to practice some deep breathing with your eyes closed. I recommend a few drops of essential oils on your hands so that you can smell the fragrance. Lavender oil is lovely and very calming to the mind.

Step 3: With your eyes closed, visualize in your mind's eye, a room that is cozy and well decorated by your creativity. This room will be called your spiritual meeting space and can be used in other meditations. In this room, add two chairs that are placed next to each other.

Step 4: Visualize yourself sitting in one of the chairs. Now, visualize your spirit appearing. It may help to see it leaving your body or walking through a door, whatever feels more natural to you. Your higher self is a spirit, the divine essence within your vessel. Allow your spirit to place its presence in the empty chair next to you. Ask questions or sit there and suck up all the warmth and beauty of what is happening. What you see is real. You have been conditioned to believe that your imagination is nothing more than a creative space for empty things. The truth is, your imagination is the key to the other side.

Step 5: After spending some time with your higher self, recite this prayer to close…..

"To my higher self, I thank you for this intimate time. Thank you for your guidance, comfort, and love. Now is the time that you return within my vessel, where I will honor you, feed you, and nurture you with love and respect. Be with me, guide me, shelter me, and show me the way." Open your eyes, blow out your candle, and give thanx! Make sure to date and document your experience in your journal.

THE AWAKENING

Step 6: Visualize your spirit self-merging within your physical self to be made back as one. To keep your spirit attached to its vessel, treat it well.

One-on-One time with your Creator (meditation)

Follow the steps in the "Opening the Connection with the Higher Self" meditation, except make some changes that will suit this connection. Keep everything the same, but this time add a doorway in your room. On top of the door, create a sign that says "My Divine Creator(s)" or any other title you choose to create for God and Goddess. As you visualize yourself seated in one chair, allow the door to open and imagine what you see as God walking through. The image of God will be different to all of us because of our own comfort, likes, and creativity. Do not get so hung up on the image, but instead document what God looks like to you, because it will reveal truths about yourself and how you view or wish God to be. Enjoy your time, ask questions, give thanx, cry, laugh, and be present.

Many people have some anger stored up towards God, and that is okay and natural. Express your emotions to your creator; you are a child of the Divine, and nothing you do is unforgivable, so be open and transparent. The only way to heal is to be present and vulnerable. I suggest performing this meditation daily or weekly to strengthen your bond with the creator. Make sure to document the experience in your journal.

Write out a personal prayer that will be used every time you choose to open communication with God. Write this prayer from your heart. It may take time, so be patient. Personal prayers are authentic and have good energy attached to them. No prayer is wrong; just be honest, straightforward, and respectful. Also, write a closing prayer that signifies that you are done with the conversation and Thankful for the time spent.

Flushing the Mind:

Reflect on negative thoughts and patterns that are stored in your mind that you wish to change. What feelings are not serving you? What negative beliefs do you have about yourself? Locate the source of these beliefs by going to your sacred space and taking time going over every thought and tracing where it came from. Do you believe you're not worthy of success, love, and happiness? Are you afraid to be courageous and go after your desires and make changes? Most of our mental patterns come from conditioning from trauma, childhood, society, and the media. Once you can identify where yours are coming from, create a plan to heal and close the door that allows these low vibrating patterns to grow. This may take some time, but once you perform this exercise, you will be flushing away the energy that keeps you connected to your pain. You will then be able to create new pathways and beliefs by initiating your plan of action. Seek a therapist or life coach if you need some help with finding your truth and creating a blueprint. You can't move forward if you are still tied to your past.

My Vessal is my Temple

Are you ready for some serious intimacy? This exercise is to help you make a genuine connection with your body and hopefully draw you closer to your divinity. This can be an intense exercise for many people that do not have a healthy relationship with their vessels, so please be kind to yourself and take your time. Our bodies are divine temples that were chosen by spirit to usher us along our journey here in the physical realm. It is through conditioning and

THE AWAKENING

the feeding of the ego that we have severed that connection and began to treat our bodies poorly. When we love something or someone, we treat them well, so maybe we should learn to love our bodies, so it's not such a struggle to be kind to ourselves. Trust the process; there is healing in the end.

Step 1: Get Naked! No one is watching, so go for it. Stand in front of a full-length mirror and take a long look. At times you may want to turn away but take a deep breath in and get back to focus. We can't heal what we run from. From head to toe, take an in-depth look at your vessel.

Step 2: Touch your hair, feel it's texture. Touch your face and glide your hands around its structure. Look and touch your hands, arms, chest, breast, and the rest of your body. This is your vessel, only society made you feel that touching and acknowledging this sacred body was wrong. You must see yourself in another light, and this will help you to shatter old beliefs and fears surrounding this connection. Continue to touch every part of you until you get to your toes.

Step 3: Back to the top, I want you to touch every part of your body again, but this time I want you to say one positive thing about every body part. I know you have it in you, and although you think you have to dig deep, the beauty is right on the surface. For you to erase what society told you about your body, you will have to create a new storyline.

Step 4: It's time to apologize. Look into your eyes, so deeply that you feel uncomfortable and move past the feeling. Take a deep breath and begin to apologize for everything you have ever done or allowed to shame your vessel. Apologize for the unhealthy foods you fed it, apologize for the toxic sexual partners you shared it with. Pour your heart out until you touch a nerve and begin to shed tears. If you have to yell, then do it, but don't walk away until you're done.

Step 5: Take a few deep breaths and center yourself. Now it's time to Thank your vessel. Thank you body for the limbs that get you from one place to the next, thank your eyes for its sight. Do a full Thank you scan from head to toe. Once you're finished, ask your body to be patient with you while you create a plan to heal and love it.

Step 6: Take a nap. Sleeping after any therapy helps the change to stick in the subconscious mind and allows you to rest well. There may be a message in your dream that will give you insight on moving forward with your healing. Once you awaken, create a plan to assist in the healing of your body. Maybe start with a book, a meal plan, or a commitment to keep away toxic partners. This is your opportunity to start new. This is where you rewrite your story.

Turn the Station

This exercise will help you identify the low vibrating people, environments, and patterns that you entertain that are keeping your frequency low. This is a straightforward exercise for you to locate any un-serving behaviors and create a plan to usher and some new ones.

Step 1: In your sacred space, make a list of all the things, people, places, and habits that are negatively impacting your desire for peace, love, success, and your purpose. This will be the low vibrating list.

Step 2: Next to all of your low vibrating items, write a positive solution for removing or changing the energy surrounding the low vibes.

The power in this exercise is being able to see what you entertain that is low vibrating and then understanding that you can solve the problem. There are some environments that we cannot avoid. Still, we can change the way we show up in those environments, and we can actively begin creating a different avenue to take instead. Remember, God, Lives within you, so there is no problem that you cannot solve, but you at least have to be open to seeing how you feed the issue at hand.

Spiritual Hearing Exercise:

To strengthen your spiritual hearing, practice silent meditation by enjoying half of your day without talking. Dedicate at least 3 hours of silence, so that you can get accustomed to hearing your inner voice. I have done this multiple times, and not only has it brought peace to my day, but it has relieved anxiety and made my spirit voice a lot louder. Write down a question that you are seeking guidance in and take it to meditation and set the intention for Spirit to answer through your spiritual hearing. You will notice that you will have some thoughts through your silent meditation when you are waiting for your answer. Spirit speaks to you through all of your senses, so if your thoughts increase or you have a bright idea, that is Spirit speaking. Write down the ideas, messages, and visions that you receive. The more you practice, the louder your message will be and the easier it will become. Try not to be so focused on what Spirit is saying, getting distracted, and keeping busy doing other things will help. Get out of your head, clean the house, organize the attic, just be silent!

Spiritual Sight Exercise:

To develop and strengthen your spiritual sight, I highly suggest daydreaming. Remember, Daydreams are visions, and no matter if you initiate the Daydream or not, Spirit will use that platform to communicate. Before even attempting to communicate with Spirit you must strengthen your spiritual sight so that you're able to see the symbols that come to you. To initiate Visions, the most natural thing that you can do is listen to music. I recommend High Vibrational music, and what that means is you want something where the melody uplifts your Spirit and creates a peaceful and calm environment. Music without lyrics will allow your mind to freely create, for words, direct your Spirit to a specific energy. You do not want to listen to anything that makes you sad, angry, anxious, or fearful. Once you have chosen your music, set an intention that you are choosing to strengthen your spiritual sight.

I suggest doing this technique for at least 5 minutes a day to start strengthening your sight. If you do this exercise every day for a week, then take the next week off and then start back up the following week. You always want to do everything in accordance to balance. Once your vision is initiated, and you begin daydreaming, allow yourself to relinquish control and just let things flow and happen as they must. When the song is over, write down your vision and close your journal.

The more you practice, you can change your intention to receive a message from Spirit. For example, if you want to know where your love life is heading, then write a clear plan before starting your exercise. If you find it difficult for a picture to appear, visualize yourself walking down a busy street. As you continue to walk, the vision will flow. Before you know it, you are in a coffee shop engaged in a conversation.

THE AWAKENING

I can feel the story

This technique will help to increase and connect with your spiritual sense of touch, also known as clairtangency.

Grab a deck of picture cards or oracle cards will do the trick. Sit in your Sacred Space and set your intentions to develop your spiritual touch. Pick one card off the top of the deck and set the others aside. Do not look at the picture on the card. Hold the card in between both hands with your eyes closed. Take a deep breath and allow your vision to bring you the energy on the card. Recite this every time you pick up a card.... "I now call to my mind's eye the image that is on this card." Do not worry about getting the image correct. Your focus should be on how your Spirit translates the image on the card. There may be a yellow duck on the card, but you may receive a dog in your vision. However, both stand for an animal. Remember, Spirit speaks a different language than what we do. The more you practice, the more you will learn to understand the way your Spirit Translate messages. Keep documentation and practice frequently. After each card, clear the space in your mind's eye by visualizing a big eraser or a stick of sage clearing the old image out so that you can welcome in the new one. This exercise also helps with spiritual knowing and seeing.

The Chameleon

Here is a technique to help empaths understand the way their senses work. You will need some friends to help you out with this one.

THE AWAKENING

Step 1: Write down at least five different emotions on paper. Each emotion has a piece of paper. Fold each piece of paper up and place them in a bowl.

Step 2: have each friend close their eyes and pick one folded piece of paper.

Step 3: ask each friend to visualize themselves as embodying the emotion on that paper. Make sure to tell them not to express the feeling on their face. For example, if one friend chose a piece of paper that says anger, she would visualize a situation that angers her. She must be careful to hide her emotions from being seen on her face.

Step 4: Once everyone has their emotion, and they are tapped into its energy, you will now choose one friend to stand in front of or hold hands for a more substantial connection. Make sure to tell your friend to continue visualizing the emotion on her piece of paper throughout the exercise.

Step 5: Close your eyes and visualize yourself merging with your friend. How do you feel? Are you angry? Are you happy? Are you sad? Speak how you feel out loud and ask your friend to validate if your emotions aligned with the paper she has chosen.

Step 6: Continue to make your way to each friend until you become more and more comfortable with the exercise and how you retrieve emotions from other people.

Step 7: When you are finished, it is imperative that you verbally speak that you wish to disconnect your connection with each person.

Example: I (name), now disconnect myself from (friends name) energy. Visualize yourself being detached from them and cleaned off by your Angels.

As an empath, you are very open to absorbing other people's emotions. When you are not disconnecting yourself from people that you have come in contact with, you will continue to carry their essence. Empaths get very confused as to what emotions are theirs and what emotions are others. This exercise identifies how easy it is to pick up on other people's energy and how quickly you believe it to be your own.

If I could change the world (Journal exercise)

Oftentimes we make finding our purpose more complicated than what it can be. During this journal exercise, you will discover things that you are passionate about that are also in connection with doing something beautiful for the world. Once you identify your passion, you're not too far from your purpose.

1- If I could change three things in the world to make it a better place, I would....

THE AWAKENING

2- If I could do these three things every day, I will feel so fulfilled in my life....

3- I hate seeing these three things done to people, animals, or the earth........

4- If I were a superhero, my power would be...........

5- The three things that stand in my way of being my best is............

Now its time for the work to be done. Take some time to meditate on the things that you have written down. How can they all come together to help heal the world? What things would you have to eliminate or transform to live your purpose? The answers that you seek are right in front of you. Take a closer look.

Dream Dictionary:

Learn the language of spirit through your dreams. Place your dream journal underneath your pillow every night, and before you get out of bed, document your drain. It is okay if you do not remember all of your dreams, just write down the things that you do recall. As your spirit gets used to you documenting your dreams, more will come to the surface. Go back and re-read what you have written down and highlight anything that grabs your attention. Maybe in your dream, you were chased by a skunk. If so, highlight the skunk. As your dreams continue to flow, the symbols will show up in your day-to-day life, and you will learn what they mean. Go back into your journal and make a note of what you have discovered the meaning is. Eventually, you will have a long list of symbols with their meanings. Hence, the next time they appear in your dream or your physical life, you can read in between the lines and receive the message.

ABOUT THE AUTHOR

Rhoni "Genesis" Le is a Prophetess, Intuitive Medium, Herbalist, and Teacher for those seeking healing and spiritual connection. She has worked with teens and adults for over ten years, assisting them in healing from trauma and discovering their spiritual gifts and power. Before working with the general public, Rhoni embarked on her journey of healing and self-acceptance, to embrace her gifts and live her purpose. She now lives a fulfilling and authentic life, raising her beautiful four children and managing her healing studio.

www.RLHealingStudio.com
HealingwithRhonile@gmail.com

THE AWAKENING

Printed in Poland
by Amazon Fulfillment
Poland Sp. z o.o., Wrocław

55826744R00056